Making Soft Toys

Karin Neuschütz

Floris Books

Translated by Susan Beard

First published as *Mjuka dockor och djur*
by Forma Books in 2012
This English edition published by Floris Books in 2012

British Library CIP Data available
ISBN 978-086315-908-4
Printed in China

Making Soft Toys

Contents

Introduction

All children, boys and girls, benefit from having dolls of their own that will take on their identity during play and help them process important events in their lives. Because dolls need help to speak, they inspire children to verbalise their feelings and expectations, dramatise their dreams and express the things they worry about, regret or desire.

Toy animals can arouse an interest in and love for the animal world, and develop feelings of protection and responsibility in the child, as well as offering possibilities for all kinds of play.

The dolls and animals in this book have simple lines and basic features, such as dots for eyes, which allow plenty of scope for the child's own imagination during play. A handmade doll or toy is unique, and an affirmation of all the time and thoughtfulness that went into making it.

The book is divided into three main sections:

1. Soft dolls and animals

Cuddly dolls to share your thoughts and worries with; to play with, feed and change. Soft animals to stroke and look after.

2. Miniature dolls and animals for a farm or zoo

Miniature dolls can be welcome additions to games and make-believe worlds. I have included a boy and a girl who visit a farm and a wildlife park, with a whole range of different animals. Being so small seems to make these dolls extra lively: they bubble with ideas and mischief. There are many fascinating stories about tiny people – think of *The Wonderful Adventures of Nils* by Selma Lagerlöf or the fairy tale *Thumbelina*. Looking through the eyes of these miniature people, children see their familiar home environment from a new perspective.

3. Glove puppets

Glove puppets are made for mischief and play-acting. They have huge potential when encouraging children to laugh and interact: the puppets want to enter into a dialogue with their audience. There is no need to create a stage or theatre – all you have to do is slip the puppet onto your hand and start telling a story! Small children are highly amused by a dog that wants to lick them or pretends to nip. Older children can use the puppets themselves and make up their own simple plays.

The patterns included here are only suggestions, and I really hope that after trying them out you will soon improve and adapt them, inventing your own designs for dolls and animals. I also hope all the sewing and playing will bring a rosy glow of enthusiasm to the cheeks of adults and children alike!

Karin Neuschütz

From left to right: two kinds of velvet, cotton fur fabric, felt, dupioni silk, raw silk, dupioni silk, fine flesh-coloured cotton knit, carded stuffing wool.

Materials, Tools and Sewing Tips

Materials

If possible choose natural fibres such as cotton, wool or silk. They are pleasant to work with and a doll or animal feels much nicer if it has been made from natural materials.

The dolls are made from fine flesh-coloured cotton knit and the clothes sewn from remnants of cotton or silk fabric. The smallest dolls and their clothes *must* be made in very thin fabric so that the pieces can be turned after sewing.

The animals are made from various types of fabric; use what you have at home or look in the fabric shop's remnant box. Choose firm fabrics or those with only a slight stretch, otherwise the animal will lose its shape when it's stuffed. Ideal fabrics are:

COTTON

Most cotton has a thin, closely woven quality such as *sheeting, flannel* or *velvet. Towelling* is cheap and suitable for larger animals, as is *table felt* (wash before use to avoid uneven shrinkage). *Cotton fur fabric* is very thin, and for *cotton knit* choose fine, plain knit for dolls' bodies.

WOOLLEN FABRIC

Always choose fine closely-woven material as it is warm and pleasant to hold. *Blanket fabric* is good for larger animals and *pure woollen fur fabric* is a fantastic material.

SILK

Silk fabric with a rough surface, such as *dupioni (Thai)*, is preferable. It's easy to work with and will not slide about. You can paint on dupioni silk using textile paints. *Raw silk* is also very easy to sew.

SYNTHETIC TEXTILES

Felt is now usually made from viscose. It's easy to work with but not especially durable. Fabric shops have a wide range of *synthetic fur* fabrics. If you decide to use synthetic fabrics then choose those that are purely cellulose, such as *viscose fur*. Fur fabric with a knitted backing is the most pliable to work with.

STUFFING

Washed and carded *sheep's wool* can be found in stores that sell supplies for Waldorf dolls (see Resources, p. 112). The curly elastic woollen fibres give this material a fantastic quality: it's washable, regains its shape and feels warm and soft.

If you want to enlarge a pattern and make a really large doll or animal, you can stuff it with a *woollen blanket* cut into strips or a *woollen jumper* rolled to fit the shape of the body and legs.

For those allergic to wool, you can use *cotton waste* (cleaning waste) or *raw cotton wool* or, if absolutely necessary, *synthetic cotton wool*. Never use pieces of foam rubber – they are dangerous for small children if the toy falls apart, and foam rubber is not as long-lasting as natural materials.

Tools

Normal sewing needle

Long thin darning needle for attaching miniature
    dolls' arms and hair

Pins

Two pairs of scissors: one for fabric, one for
    paper (fabric scissors will become blunt if
    used for cutting paper)

Sewing thread in the same colours as the fabrics

Tape measure

Thimble

Soft pencil or marking pen

Felting needle and foam rubber base (bath sponge)

Blunt chopstick, plant stick or barbecue skewer
    for turning and stuffing

Sewing machine with straight and zigzag stitch,
    and preferably stretch-stitch

Textile pen or embroidery silk for the eyes etc.

Sewing tips

Dolls

Make them from thin stretchy cotton knit. It's easiest if you cut out the paper templates *without* a seam allowance (that is, following the dotted line). Draw round them on double fabric with the knit running vertically, leaving room around the edge for a seam allowance. Sew along the drawn line. Sew *before* you cut out the pieces.

Sew using sewing machine needle size 70 (10)

Always try the clothes on the doll when sewing
    them!

'Fold' beside a broken line indicates that the
    pattern is half the piece; it has been folded as
    a mirror image. Place the pattern on double
    fabric with the broken line against the fold
    (see p. 12, Figure 1).

Animals

Pin the pattern templates on the wrong side of single fabric, making sure the direction with most stretch runs horizontally across the animal. Woven fabric stretches most on the diagonal. When sewing an animal in fur fabric check that the fur runs in a natural direction: that is, downwards on the body sides and up towards the forehead on the nose gusset (marked with arrows on the pattern, see rabbit, p. 40).

Note that the side and the underneath of the
    body should be drawn once facing left and
    once facing right.

Key to pattern lines

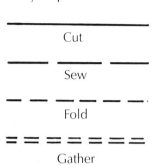

Cut

Sew

Fold

Gather

1

2

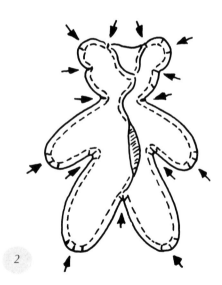

3

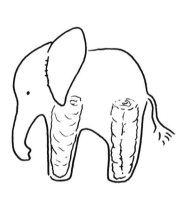

4

Ladder-stitch

5

12

Tack velvet and fur fabric before you sew, otherwise the pieces will slip.

Most seams can be sewn on a machine using a small zigzag or stretch-stitch. It's best to sew tricky sections such as nose gussets and ears by hand.

Make sure the seams are in the right place on the reverse side as well.

Trimming means cutting away unnecessarily wide seam allowances and making small notches or cuts in the seam allowance in all places that might be difficult to turn: for example, ear folds, at the neck, under the arms, the ends of paws and between the legs (Figure 2).

Use a chopstick for help when stuffing. Fill firmly as the wool will compact over time. Fill the head of an animal before the nose so that the stuffing inside the head will hold the small wool ball of the nose in place (Figure 3).

Fill the legs of the animals with bound 'rods' of wool, longer than the actual leg (Figure 4). Then add wool to fill the space between the upper ends of the rods to prevent the legs from bending outwards.

Sew up the animal's opening with ladder-stitch (Figure 5).

Washing

It's best to wash toys that are stuffed with wool by hand in lukewarm water. Rub gently with a sponge, using a little soap or shampoo. Rinse thoroughly and squeeze tightly in a towel to press out excess water. Massage the toy back into shape. Allow to dry in a warm and airy place. Children usually enjoy bathing dolls and animals, and this is a good way for them to learn how to keep them clean.

Soft Dolls

MATERIALS
Flesh-coloured cotton knit
Stuffing wool
Fine woollen yarn for hair
Sewing thread for eyes, mouth and stitching
Strong thread for tying

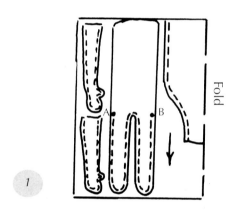

1

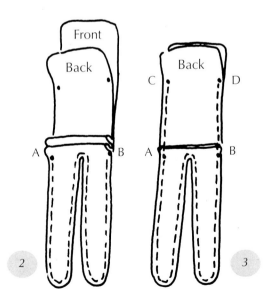

2   *3*

It's lovely to have a warm, soft doll to talk to and hug. Here are Lisa and Kim, both made from the same simple pattern. The finished doll is 20–25 cm (8–10 in) tall. The pattern has been shrunk by 10 percent to fit the page of this English-language edition.

Photocopy the pattern on page 16, enlarging by 10 percent. A bigger doll can be made by enlarging the pattern further, but in that case remember to enlarge the clothes patterns as well.

Cut out the enlarged, photocopied pattern along the *dotted* line. Draw around the pieces on double fabric, leaving space for seam allowances and making sure the ribbing runs vertically.

Sew the pieces before you cut them out using a narrow zigzag or stretch-stitch along the drawn line. Sew around the arms, leaving them open at the top. Sew the head flap, leaving it open at the top and the bottom. On the body piece sew only from A to B around the legs (Figure 1).

Cut out all the pieces. Make two upward-facing folds immediately above points A and B on one body piece (the back) (Figure 2). This will give the doll a bottom, so it can sit well. Make the folds about ½ cm (¼ in) deep. Pin and sew the folds in place, stitching along each side up to the marks for the arms, from A to C and B to D. Leave an opening at each side and at the top for the arms. Trim the front piece to make it the same length as the back piece (Figure 3). Trim all the pieces, cutting small notches at the groin and the thumb join, and turn the pieces the right way out.

Using stuffing wool, form a hard ball by winding small strips as if winding yarn into a ball. Wind

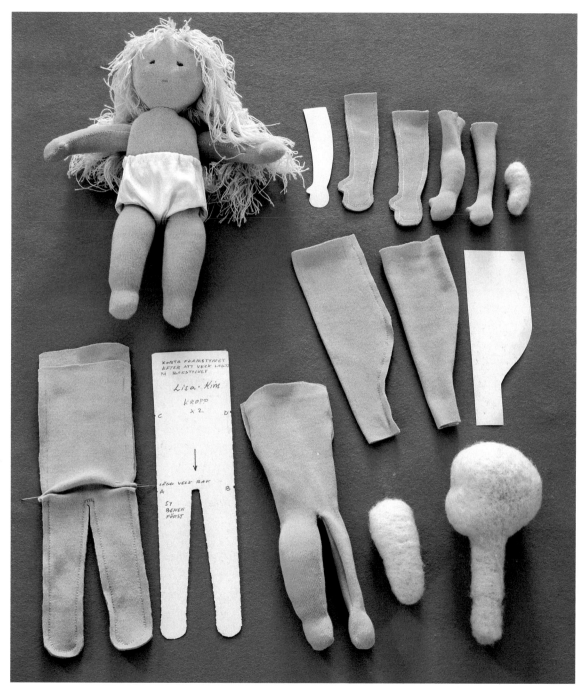

You can see in the photo that the pattern is cut out along the dotted line. The stitched body shows the two tucks in the back piece. With the felted parts, the arm is shorter than the fabric arm piece. A felting needle is used to mould the head's facial features.

SOFT DOLL

Note: This pattern has been reduced by 10 percent to fit this book's page size. Photocopy, enlarging by 10 percent.

Shorten the front piece after folds have been made on the back piece

LISA AND KIM
BODY x 2

C

D

Make folds in back piece

A

B

Sew the legs first

Leave open

LISA AND KIM
HEAD x 1

Fold

Leave open

LISA AND KIM
ARM x 4

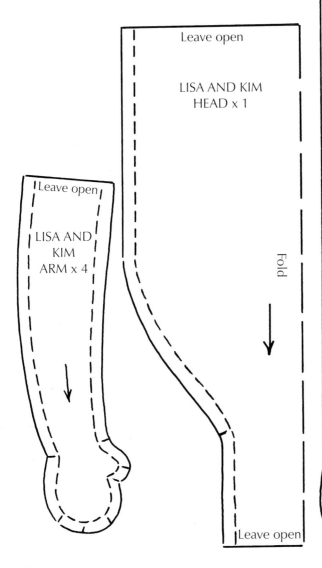
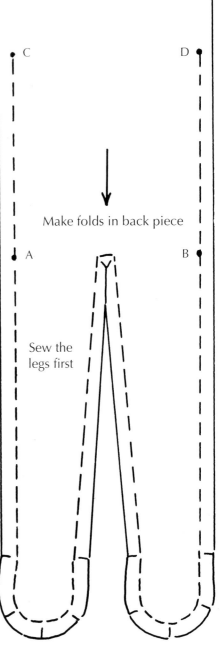

in different directions (Figure 4). Secure the strips from time to time with a felting needle. When the ball is about 6 cm (2½ in) in diameter and fairly solid, place it on two thin, wide strips of wool placed at right angles (Figure 5) and wrap the wool around the head ball (Figure 6).

Wind a thin strip of wool around the neck as close to the head ball as you can. Wind tightly around the front and the back of the neck until the head feels stable, but keep the neck narrow (Figure 7). Using the felting needle attach several small layers of wool to form the back of the head, the chin and the cheeks (Figure 8).

Shape the head and face with the help of the felting needle. Stab the needle into the wool repeatedly in the places where you want the surface to be indented. The head must feel solid, with a circumference of about 20 cm (8 in). Make the forehead high (half the head) to give the doll a childlike look. If you like you can roll a very small ball of wool (the size of a pea) for a nose, which you can attach with a thin strip of wool (Figure 9). Carefully even out the face with the felting needle: all the wool must be firmly secured.

Cover the head with the head fabric, pulled on from beneath so that the neck slots into the narrow end (Figure 10). Trim away any surplus fabric at the top (Figure 11). Stretch the fabric up and back from the face and join on top of the head, sewing it in place. Wind strong thread, such as rug warp, around the neck immediately below the chin, pull tight and tie at the neck (Figure 12).

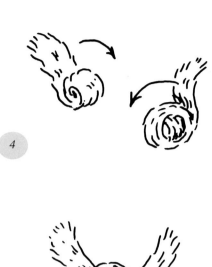

4

5

6

7

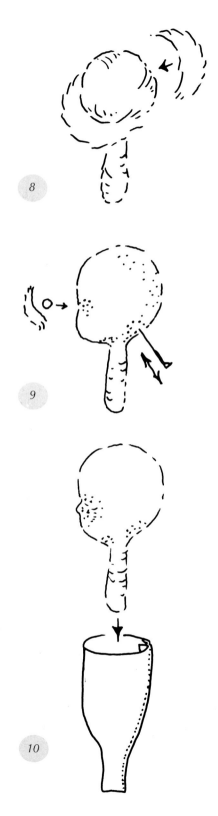

8

9

10

Take two equal-sized tufts of wool to stuff the hands and then repeat for the feet, using a chopstick to help you (Figure 13). Fold a strip of wool so that it's slightly shorter than the leg fabric (Figure 14). Wind thin strips of wool tightly around this inner layer so that the leg feels stable; this will make the wool leg a little longer (Figure 15). Measure it against the fabric leg to make sure it's the same size. Fasten the wool occasionally with a felting needle. Make the leg thicker at the top to shape the thigh. Wind firmly, pulling tight all the time so that the leg will be firm and solid. A baby's legs can be slightly bowed (Figure 16).

Do the same with the arms but note that the arm inserts are not as long as the fabric they will be inserted into (Figure 17). Make the arms thinner than the legs. When you have made two identical arms and two legs you can smooth out any unevenness with the felting needle, making the pairs as similar as possible. Insert the woollen arms and legs into the fabric. The arms will not fill all the fabric: the upper third will be empty. The legs will reach all the way up to the groin.

Now lay the empty arm fabric against the neck and attach the fabric so that the thumb faces forwards (Figure 18). Attach the second arm to the other side of the neck. Check to make sure the arms are the same length (Figure 19).

Wind a thin layer of wool over each shoulder and many strips around the chest and back (Figure 20). Wind plenty of layers around the stomach to make it rounded. Prepare a thin, wide strip of wool to cover the entire body (Figure 21). Secure the wool with the felting needle around the doll's bottom and stomach (Figure 22). Make the body about $1^{1}/_{2}$ times the length of the head.

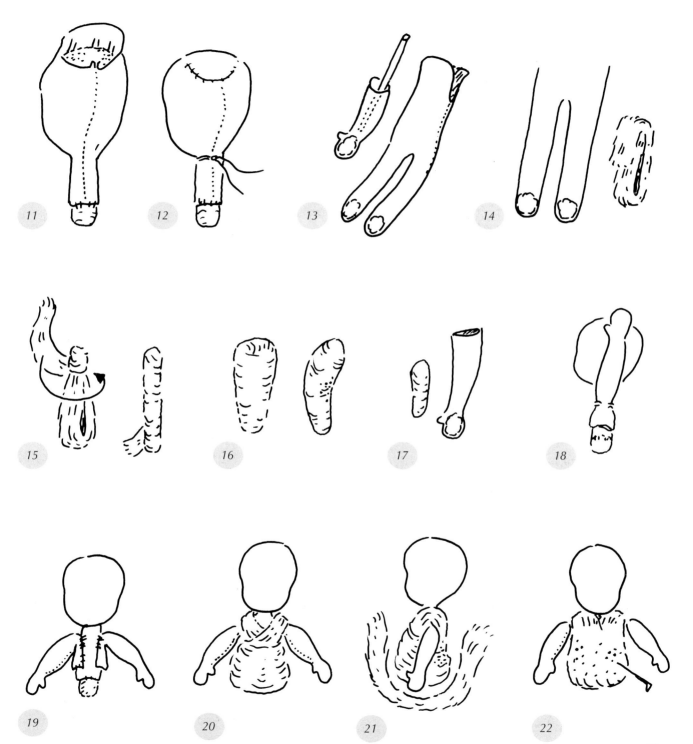

11   12   13   14

15   16   17   18

19   20   21   22

Insert the body into the fabric and arrange the wool. Pull away or push in any wool that protrudes at the top. Fold in the seam allowance on the front piece and stretch it up to the chin. Insert a pin into the fabric on each side of the neck, pushing them downwards into the fabric to hold it in place. Do the same with the back piece (Figure 23).

Fasten the front and back pieces of fabric onto the shoulders as close to the head as possible. Then using ladder-stitch, sew around the neck so that the fabric is attached immediately above the strong thread tied round the neck. Now sew the shoulder seams together, folding in more fabric furthest out to give the shoulders a slight slope. Check that the hole around the arms fits snugly. If the armhole is too large you can make the side seam longer. Make the arm attachments as small as possible so that the doll's arms will be flexible and survive all the pulling about when being dressed and undressed. Sew a little dot for the navel.

Insert pins to mark the position of the eyes and mouth so that they form an equilateral triangle. Choose a natural fibre sewing thread for the eyes: sewing cotton, pearl silk, buttonhole silk or the finest embroidery wool. Insert a long thin darning needle into the side of the head (Figure 24). Leaving the end of the thread inside the head, push the needle out where the eye will be. Sew a couple of stitches in the same place, count the number and repeat for the other eye. The needle then exits on the other side of the head. The mouth is stitched after the eyes using sewing cotton. You can also use a textile pen to mark the eyes and mouth if you prefer.

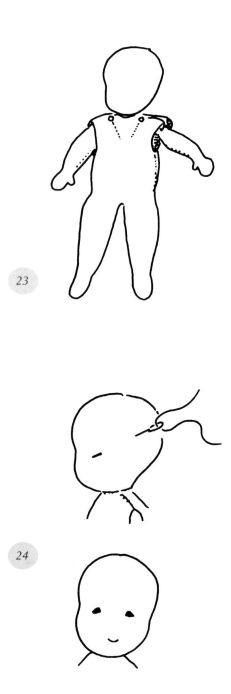

23

24

Hairstyles

LISA

ELLIE

Choose fine woollen weaving or worsted yarn.

LISA'S HAIR

First cut long lengths of yarn to use for attaching the hair. Then make a basic layer of hair by cutting enough strands of yarn to form a fringe and a layer running over the head and down to the desired length at the back (Figure 1). Place the strands on the head, hold in place at the hairline and lift up the fringe. Check the doll's forehead is high enough – a high forehead looks more childlike. Sew a horizontal seam with small back-stitches along the hairline. Comb the hair back with the help of the needle so that the strands lie parallel and then sew three or four more parallel horizontal rows (Figure 2). The last row of stitches will form the hairline at the nape of the neck, about 1 cm (½ in) up from the neck seam. Add more yarn around the ears if necessary. Cut several layers of yarn long enough to reach from the bottom of the hair, partially up the back of the

head and down again. Sew the strands in place with two horizontal rows of stitching, the bottom row a centimetre or two above the lower hairline. Carry on in this way all around the back of the head (Figure 3). Finally place a layer of strands at right angles across the base hair layer and sew in place, forming a centre parting, followed by two further seams parallel to the parting (Figure 4).

ELLIE'S HAIR

Embroider long stitches from the hairline towards the middle of the crown (Figure 1), by making small stitches into the fabric and longer stitches on the outside (Figure 2). When the whole of the crown has been covered, make loops to form tousled, rather sparse hair (Figure 3). Begin at the hairline around the head by sewing first a short stitch followed by a long one, making a loose loop of the desired length, followed by a small fastening stitch again, and so on, at roughly 1 cm (½ in) intervals (Figure 4). Continue around the

entire head until it is covered with floppy loops. Then cut through the loops (Figure 5).

Sam's hair

First cut lengths to use for sewing, then cut strands of yarn to reach across the head from side to side to the desired length (Figure 1). Attach this layer of hair by stitching a centre parting, combing it down on each side and bringing it together at the back (Figure 2). Attach it at the hairline at the nape of the neck. Cut strands of yarn long enough to reach from the bottom to halfway up the head and down again. Hold these strands in place with two horizontal rows of stitching, one about 1–2 cm ($^1/_2$–$^3/_4$ in) above the lower hairline and a parallel one about 2 cm ($^3/_4$ in) above it (Figure 3). Finish by cutting another layer of strands to reach across the head at right angles and down to the desired length on either side. Attach this layer to all the hair by sewing a centre parting and a seam on either side of it (Figure 4).

Kim's hair

Cut several long strands to sew with. Crochet the yarn (use several threads at a time; it will be quicker), wet it and let it dry. Undo the crocheted yarn and it will be curly. Place all the curly yarn in a pile and spread it out randomly over the doll's head (Figure 1). Attach it with stitches dotted here and there over the whole scalp. Fasten especially well around the hairline (Figure 2). Cover any places where the scalp shows through with embroidered stitches.

Mia's hair

Cut suitable lengths and use them to embroider long stitches all over the scalp from the place where the centre parting will be round to two points at the back of the head where the plaits will start (Figure 1). Leave long loose ends at these two points, and leave equally long ends at these points when you start with a new piece

LISA

1

2

3

4

ELLIE

1

2

3

4

5

SAM

1

2

3

4

23

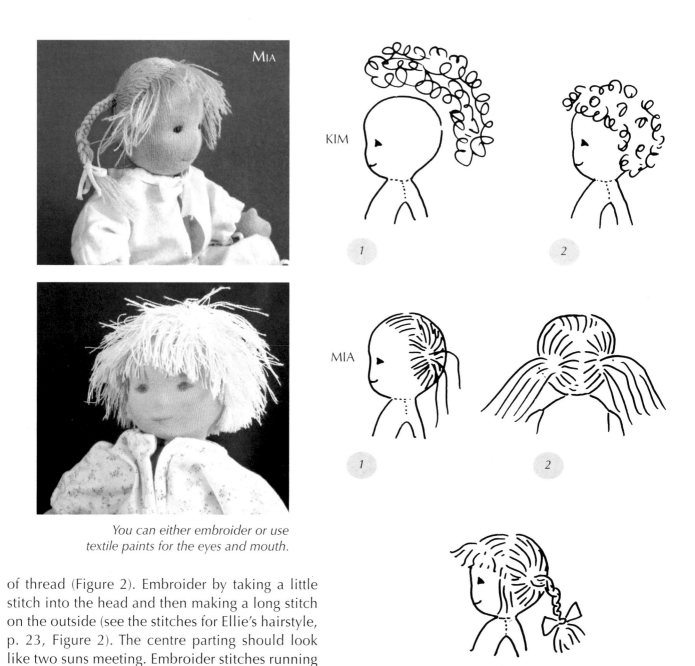

MIA

KIM

1

2

MIA

1

2

3

You can either embroider or use textile paints for the eyes and mouth.

of thread (Figure 2). Embroider by taking a little stitch into the head and then making a long stitch on the outside (see the stitches for Ellie's hairstyle, p. 23, Figure 2). The centre parting should look like two suns meeting. Embroider stitches running forwards, the ends forming a fringe (Figure 3). Plait long loose ends, tie with ribbon.

24

Clothes for Lisa and Kim

The clothes are made using *thin* double fabric, preferably cotton or dupioni silk. It is easiest to sew with double material because then you avoid the fiddly job of edging or hemming sleeves, legs and openings. But you can of course use single fabric if you want to go to that trouble!

DRESS/CAMISOLE

Trace the pattern from page 26 onto paper, cut it out and measure it against the doll to see if it fits. Lay it on double fabric with the wrong side facing out (you can have one fabric for an outer layer and a different fabric for the lining). Draw round the pattern with a pencil. Pin then sew following the dotted line on the pattern, leaving an opening to allow for turning right side out (p. 26, Figure 1). Cut out, cutting small notches around the armholes and neck. Turn the work, pushing out the straps with the help of a chopstick. Press.

Now you can sew a decorative row a short way in from the edge, at the same time sewing up the opening. Sew the straps together with a few stitches at the top by hand. Try it on and mark the position of the press fasteners or hooks and eyes at the back and sew them in place.

TIPS

Sew the lining in a different colour.

If the dress is to have pockets, sew them onto the right side of the outer fabric before it is attached to the lining.

When shortened the pattern can be used to make a camisole.

UNDERPANTS

Trace and cut out the paper pattern from page 27, try it against the doll and adjust if necessary. Draw round the template on double fabric, wrong side out. Measure the doll's waist and adjust the pattern. Sew following the dotted line, leaving openings for drawstrings and for turning right side out (Figure 1). Cut out, turn and stitch up the opening. Sew the channel for the drawstring front and back (Figure 2). Fold the panties double and stitch the sides (Figure 3). Thread narrow elastic through the waist.

TIPS

Add a layer of felt or a thin layer of wool before you sew the fabric and lining together to make training panties.

DUNGAREES/OVERALLS

Trace the pattern from page 29 onto paper and cut it out. Try it against the doll and make adjustments. Draw the pattern twice on the wrong side of the outer fabric and twice on the lining. Cut out the pocket and fold it with right sides facing and sew around it, leaving an opening for turning. Turn and attach the pocket to one of the front pieces of the outer fabric. Lay the outer fabric against the lining, right sides facing.

Pin and sew around both pieces of the dungarees before you cut them out. Leave an opening for turning (p. 30, Figure 1). Trim the pieces, cutting notches in the seam allowance at every corner. Turn and push out the straps. Sew up the opening on the legs. Fold the legs one at a

LISA'S DRESS

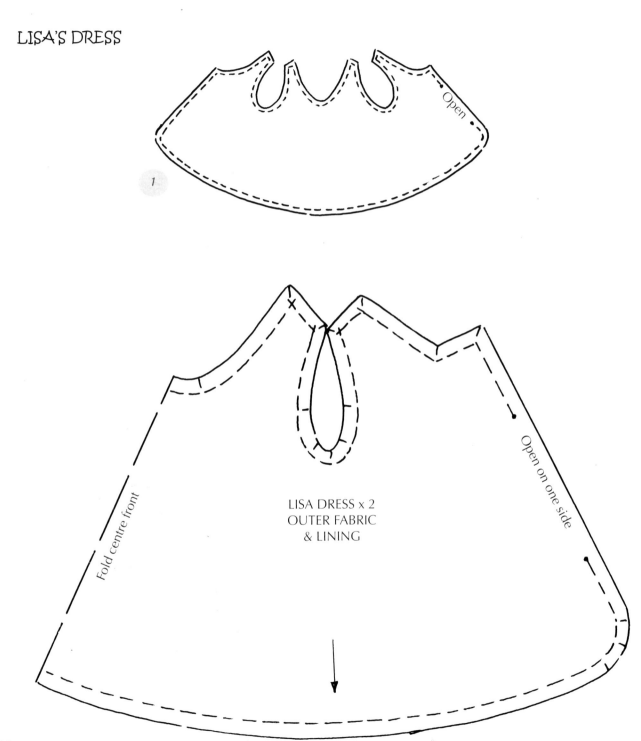

Open

1

Fold centre front

Open on one side

LISA DRESS x 2
OUTER FABRIC
& LINING

26

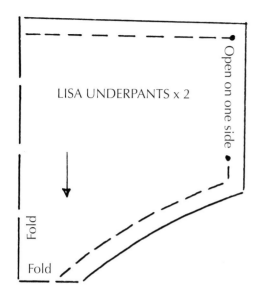

LISA UNDERPANTS x 2

Open on one side

Fold

Fold

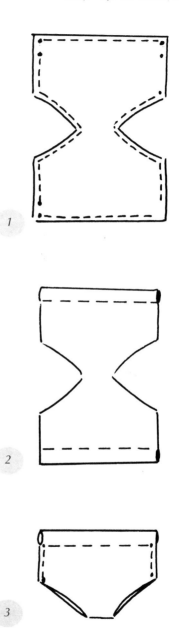

time, right sides facing, and then sew the legs up to the groin (Figure 2).

Turn one leg so that the right side faces out and insert it into the other leg. Sew the back seam down to the crotch and up over the stomach as far as you choose (Figure 3). Turn right side out. Try the dungarees on and attach the buttons and fastenings on the straps (see photo, p. 28).

TIP

You can make overalls from the same pattern. Attach sleeves that have also been sewn in double fabric (see pattern, p. 29). If the doll is for a very young child it might be a good idea to sew the overalls to the doll around the neck, wrists and ankles, otherwise the doll will often be left naked and cold!

DUNGAREES/OVERALLS

Centre front and back

KIM DUNGAREES x 4
(OVERALLS)
OUTER FABRIC x 2
LINING x 2

Fold

Shorts

Open on one side

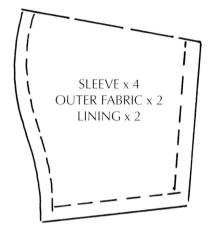

SLEEVE x 4
OUTER FABRIC x 2
LINING x 2

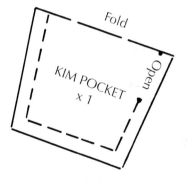

Fold

Open

KIM POCKET
x 1

KIM'S DUNGAREES

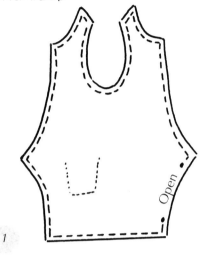

Open

1

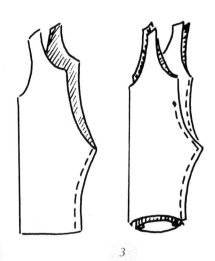

2   3

Shirt/nightdress

Trace the pattern from page 31 onto paper and cut it out. Try it against the doll and adjust. Draw around the template on double fabric, right sides facing. Sew along the drawn line. Leave an opening for turning (p. 31, Figure 1). Cut out, making small notches in the seam allowance around the neck and armholes. Turn right side out and press.

Fold in the seam allowance at the opening and sew a decorative row around all the edges of the shirt, sewing up the opening at the same time. Fold the shirt, right sides facing, and sew the side and sleeve seams. Sew on buttons or hooks and eyes (Figure 2).

TIP

At the same time as you sew the lining and outer fabric together, you can sew a lace edging at the bottom. If you decide to do this, make sure the lace is between the fabrics on the inside.

If the sleeves are too long and the shirt too wide you can make a couple of tucks over the shoulders running about 3 cm (1 in) down the front and back pieces.

You can lengthen the shirt to make it into a nightdress.

SHIRT/NIGHTDRESS

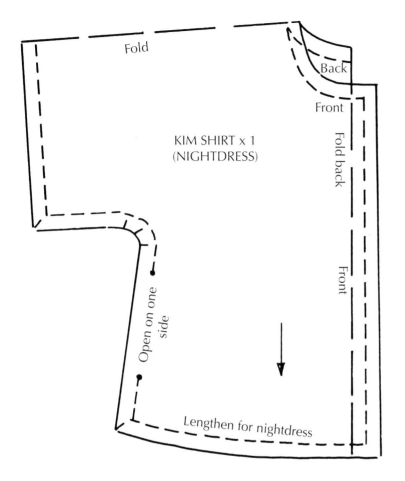

Fold

Back

Front

KIM SHIRT x 1
(NIGHTDRESS)

Fold back

Front

Open on one side

Lengthen for nightdress

Open

1

2

Soft Animals

Teddy bear

MATERIALS
Fake fur fabric, preferably natural fibre
Stuffing wool
Yarn to embroider eyes and nose

Trace the pattern pieces from pages 36 and 37, cut them out and draw round them on the wrong side of the fabric. Check that the direction of the fur runs downwards on the body and limbs and upwards on the face. You will have one front and one back body piece, two left-facing and two right-facing arms and the same for the legs, two head pieces, plus one face and one back of head piece.

Cut out the 14 pieces. Place the head side pieces together, right sides facing. Pin, tack and sew following the dotted line from A to B, nose to throat (p. 34, Figure 1).

Place the back of head piece against the face piece, right sides facing. Pin, tack and stitch around the ears from C to C (Figure 2). Insert the stitched face and neck piece between the head sides. Pin, tack and sew from the nose A, up to the ear C, and round to the neck D, on both sides (Figure 3). Turn the head right side out.

Lay the arm and the leg pieces together in pairs, right sides facing. Pin, tack and stitch them, leaving an opening at the top to turn them (Figure 4). Turn the arms and legs right side out and stuff them. Pinch their openings together, seam against seam, and tack (Figure 5).

This doll has been made from the pattern on page 16, enlarged by an extra 50 percent, and the overalls from the pattern on page 29, enlarged by 50 percent.

Sew together the three slits at the bottom of the front piece and the back piece (Figure 6). Place the front and back pieces together, right sides facing. Pin and stitch the shoulder seams and the straight sides. Leave a gap for the arms (Figure 7).

Insert an arm between the front and back so that the paw faces in towards the stomach and the upper part of the arm peeps out through the body's armhole. Attach the arm with strong thread. Repeat with the other arm (Figure 8).

Work the (empty) head, turned right side out, upside down into the body so that the head's throat opening lies inside the throat opening of the body fabric. Check that the nose is pointing in the same direction as the stomach and that the back of head gusset is centre back. Sew them together around the neck by hand with strong thread (Figure 9).

Turn the body piece right side out – the head and arms are now in place. Lay one leg upside down on the stomach fabric so that the toes point towards the nose. Attach the leg to the body, sewing by hand with strong thread. Repeat for the other leg (Figure 10). Fold the legs down.

Stuff the head full before forming the nose from a small hard ball of stuffing. Stuff the body firmly, giving it a rounded shape. Sew the opening together (Figure 11).

The eyes can be sewn with embroidery thread or another kind of brown or black yarn. Use dark brown yarn for the nose and mouth. For positioning, see Figure 12.

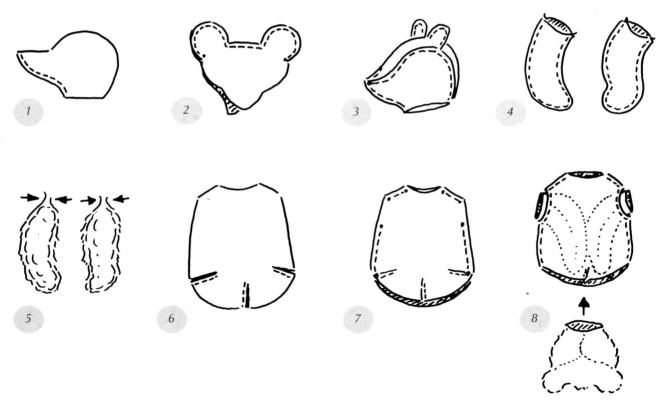

9

10

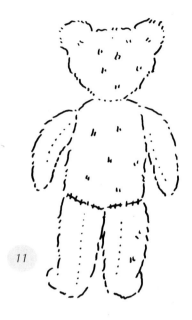

11

Too high up

Too close together

Too far apart

Just right!

12 POSITION OF
FACIAL DOTS

TEDDY BEAR

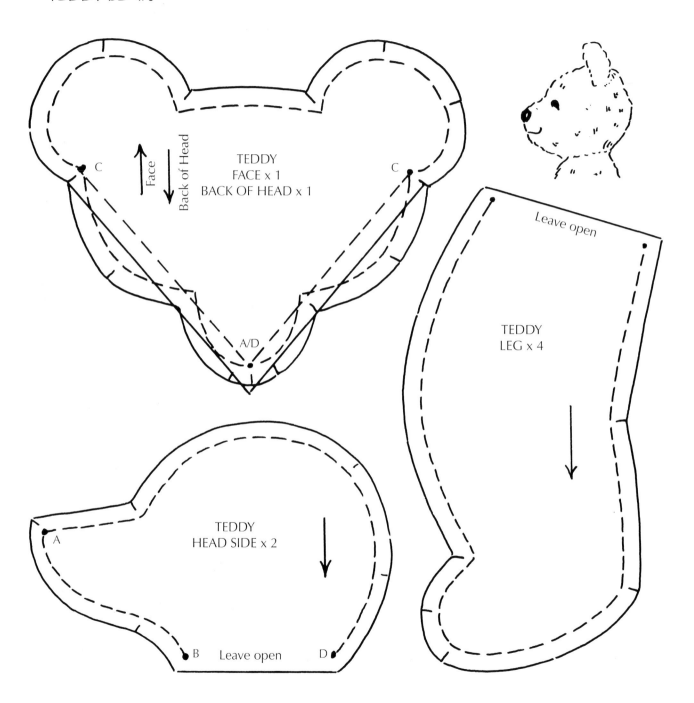

TEDDY
FACE x 1
BACK OF HEAD x 1

Face

Back of Head

C

C

A/D

TEDDY
LEG x 4

Leave open

TEDDY
HEAD SIDE x 2

A

B   Leave open   D

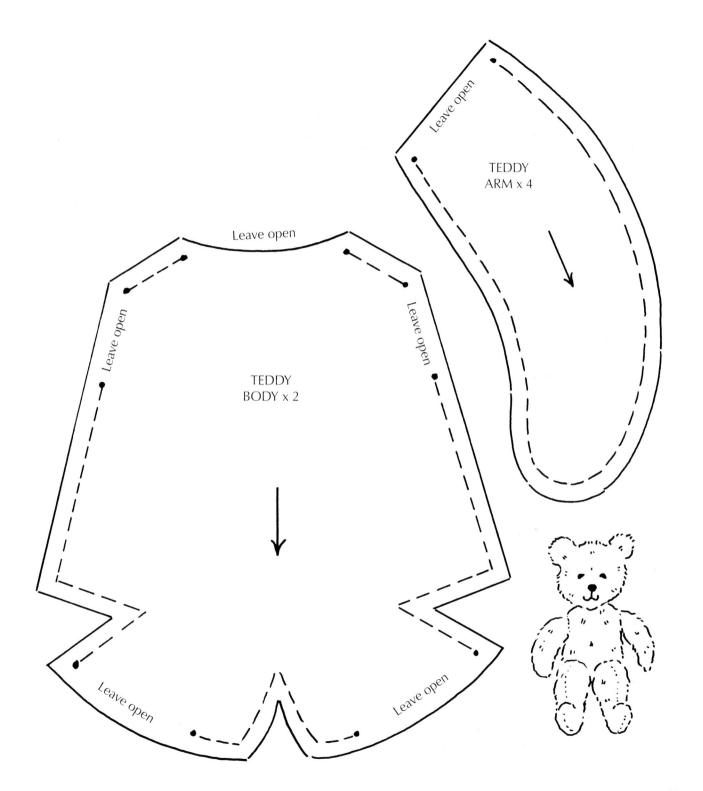

TEDDY
ARM x 4

Leave open

TEDDY
BODY x 2

Leave open

Leave open

Leave open

Leave open

Leave open

Rabbit

MATERIALS
Fur fabric, preferably woollen
Pink felt for inside ears
Stuffing wool
Yarn for embroidering eyes

Trace the pattern pieces from page 40 onto paper and cut them out. Lay the templates on the wrong side of the fabric and draw round them in pencil. There will be one left and one right body part, two underneath pieces, two main fur ears plus two pink ear-linings, a nose gusset and a tail. Cut out the pieces.

Place each ear piece together with its pink lining, right sides facing. Pin and sew round, leaving an opening at the base. Turn the ears. They will not be stuffed and will be folded together at the base when attached to the head (Figure 1).

Fold the tail piece and sew it together, right sides facing. Turn and stuff with a little wool (Figure 2). Lay the body sides together, right sides facing. Pin and stitch from A to B. Insert the stuffed tail between the side pieces immediately above D. Make sure it is turned right side out and faces inwards into the body. Pin and stitch the back seam C to D, fixing the tail in place at the same time (Figure 3).

Sew the nose gusset into place. Begin on one side and sew from A up over the head. When the seam turns down towards the back of the neck insert one of the ears, turned right side out,

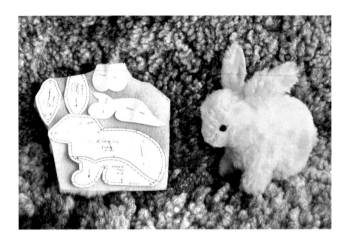

making sure it points inwards into the head with only a small amount of the folded-over base of the ear protruding. Finish sewing the seam down to C, at the same time fixing the ear in place. Do the same with the other side of the face and the second ear (Figure 4).

Place the underneath pieces together, right sides facing, and sew from B to D, (Figure 5). Spread open the rabbit's paws and insert the underneath piece, right sides facing. Pin and sew round the paw from B to E on both sides. Now the rabbit is open only between E and D (Figure 6). Turn the work right side out, stuff the rabbit firmly and sew the opening together by hand.

Embroider large round eyes in dark brown yarn. If you have made the rabbit in fur fabric the face can be trimmed a little by cutting away the fur around the nose.

1

2

3

4

5

6

RABBIT

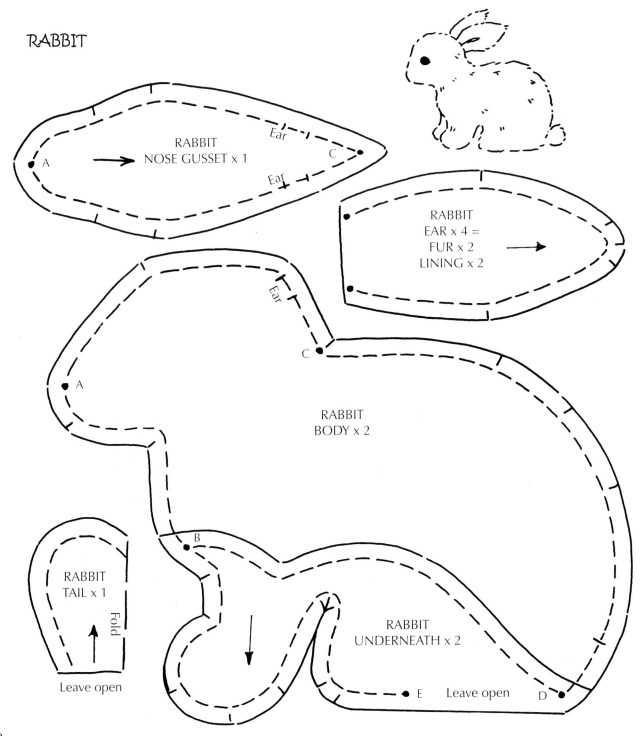

RABBIT
NOSE GUSSET x 1

A

Ear

C

Ear

RABBIT
EAR x 4 =
FUR x 2
LINING x 2

Ear

C

A

RABBIT
BODY x 2

B

RABBIT
TAIL x 1

Fold

Leave open

RABBIT
UNDERNEATH x 2

E   Leave open   D

Cat and fox

MATERIALS FOR CAT
Fur fabric or velvet
Stuffing wool
Yarn for nose, eyes and whiskers

MATERIALS FOR RED FOX
White and reddish-brown fur fabric
Stuffing wool
Yarn for nose and eyes

Trace the pattern pieces from pages 44 and 45 onto paper and cut them out. Draw round the pieces on the wrong side of the fabric so that the direction of the fur follows the arrows on the pattern. Cut out all the pieces.

Red fox: Fox is pictured on page 76, and see Figures 1 and 2, this page. Sew the side pieces and the tail together first: pin and sew together one body piece at a time with its cheek piece, right sides facing, from A to B (Figure 3). Place the white tail tip on the red tail, right sides facing, and stitch from G to H (Figure 4).

From now on follow the same instructions for both cat and fox. Place the face and neck together, right sides facing. Pin and sew the ears together by hand from C to D (Figure 5). Place the underneath pieces together, right sides facing, pin and sew from E to F (Figure 6). Place the body sides together, right sides facing, and sew from nose to chest, J to E, and down the back, K to L (Figure 7).

RED FOX

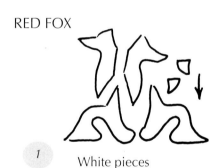

1 White pieces

2 Reddish-brown pieces

Place the stitched head piece between the cheeks, right sides facing, and sew by hand from the nose to the back of the head, J to K, on each side (Figure 8). Fit the underneath piece between the legs of the body piece, pin and sew from E to M around the legs on each side (Figure 9).

Trim the seam allowance and cut small notches in all sharp angles. Turn right side out and push out the pieces with the help of a chopstick. Sew a couple of stitches in the middle of the base of the ears through both layers of fabric to prevent them being filled when you stuff the head. Stuff with wool, first the head and then the nose and so on down to the throat. Make two leg shapes (see the doll's arms on p. 19) longer than the leg fabric and push them into the fabric. Fill in the gaps between the inserted leg shapes that protrude into the body so that the animal's paws will hold together well. Stuff the entire body.

Insert the tail, sewing it in place between L and F, and stitch up the opening underneath (Figure 10).

Embroider eyes closer to the nose than the ears. Cats have a small light brown or pink nose; foxes have a large black or brown nose. Give them both whiskers.

Tip

Make the small fox on the pattern page in the same way. It goes with the animals on the farm or in the wildlife park (see page 76).

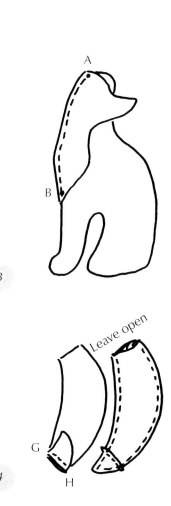

3

4

5

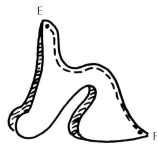

6

7

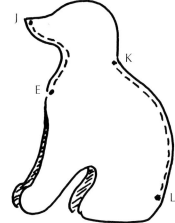

8

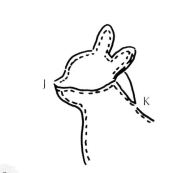

9

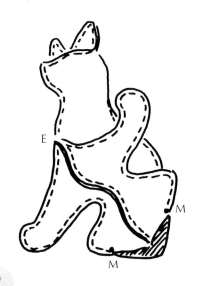

10

43

CAT/FOX

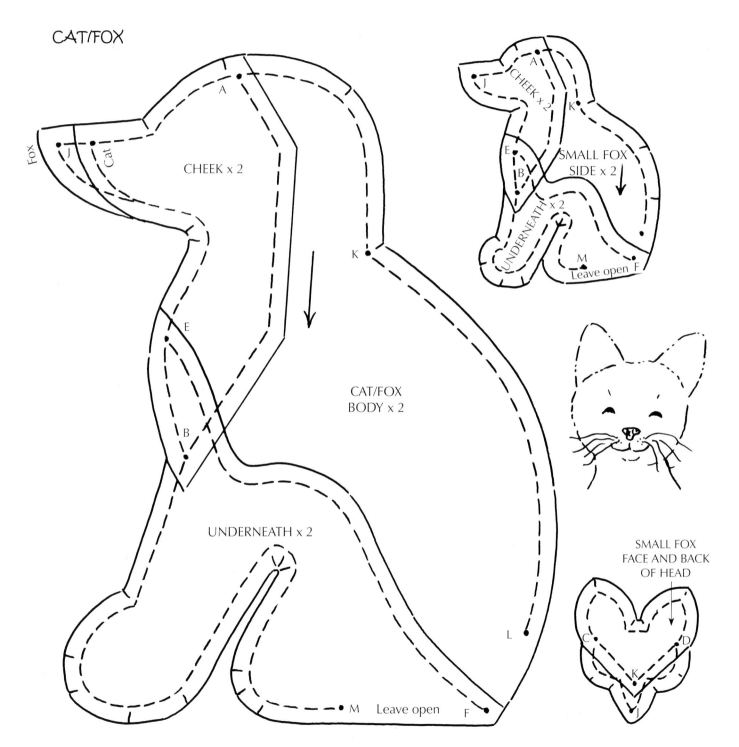

CHEEK x 2

Fox

Cat

J

A

CHEEK x 2

A

J

K

E

B

SMALL FOX
SIDE x 2

UNDERNEATH x 2

M

Leave open   F

K

E

B

CAT/FOX
BODY x 2

UNDERNEATH x 2

L

M   Leave open   F

SMALL FOX
FACE AND BACK
OF HEAD

C

D

K

J

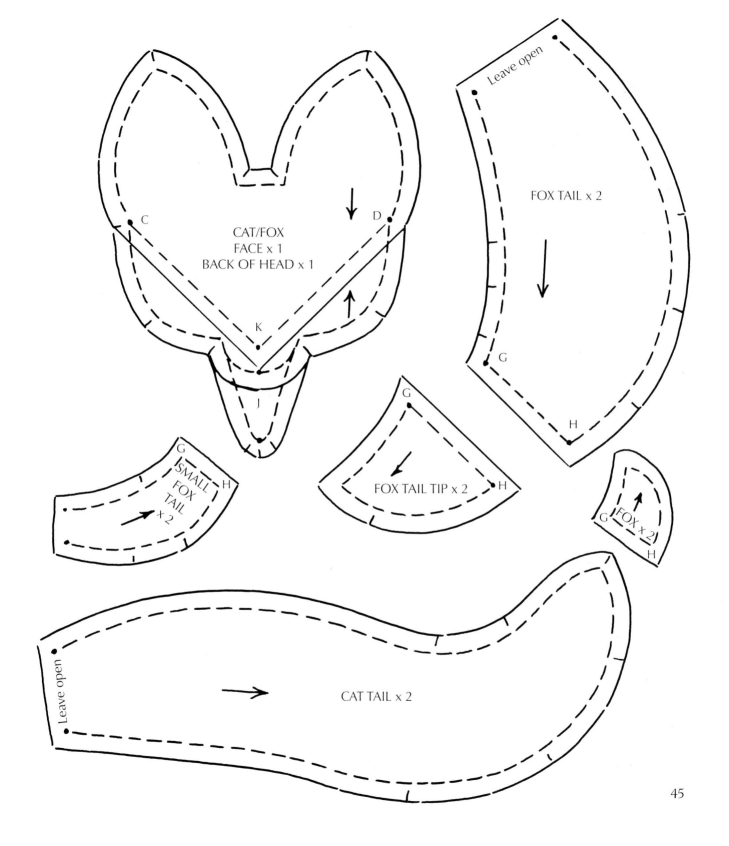

CAT/FOX
FACE x 1
BACK OF HEAD x 1

C

D

K

J

FOX TAIL x 2

G

H

G

FOX TAIL TIP x 2

H

Leave open

SMALL
FOX
TAIL
x 2

G

H

G

FOX x 2

H

Leave open

CAT TAIL x 2

45

Kitten

MATERIALS

Felt or velvet; for the small kitten, dupioni silk
Stuffing wool
Sewing thread for eyes, nose, mouth and whiskers

Trace the pattern from page 47 onto paper and cut it out. Draw round the pieces so you have one right-facing and one left-facing body piece, plus two underneath pieces. Place the body halves together right sides facing. The little cat is sewn by hand.

Pin and stitch the front of the face from A to B. Take care with the small protruding nose section. Sew the neck, back and tail, from C to D (Figure 1). Bring A up to C on top of the head and sew together, first in the middle between the ears, then one ear at a time (Figure 2).

Place the underneath pieces right sides together, pin and stitch the stomach seam but leave the middle third open for turning (Figure 3). Fold the legs on one body side up towards the body and insert the underneath piece, right sides facing. Pin and sew round the legs from B to D first on one side, then the other (Figure 4).

Check that all the seams look secure on the reverse side. Trim around all pieces and cut small notches in the seam allowance as indicated on the pattern. Turn and stuff the cat. Make sure the cheeks are filled out so that the head is rounded. Sew up the opening in the stomach with small slip-stitches. Embroider or draw eyes and nose, and make whiskers using sewing thread.

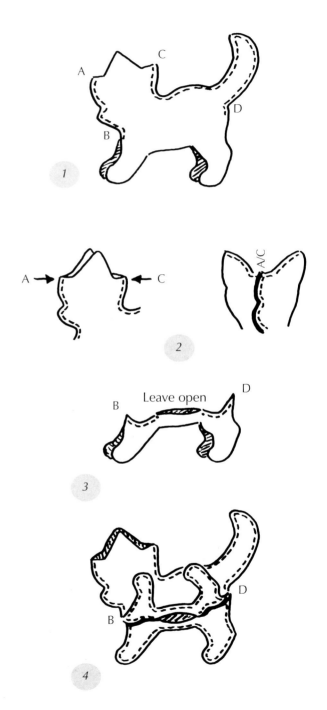

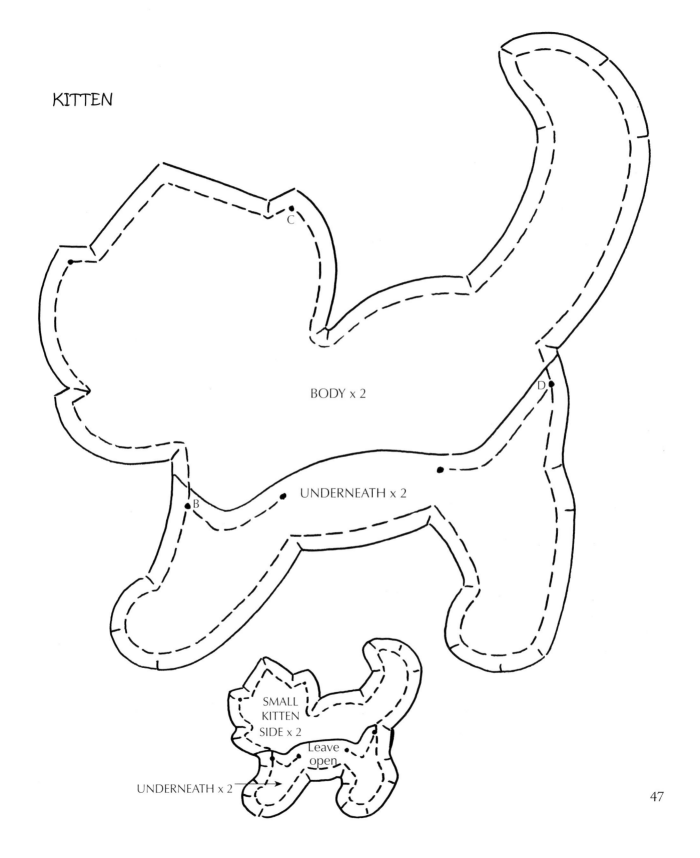

KITTEN

BODY x 2

C

D

B

UNDERNEATH x 2

SMALL
KITTEN
SIDE x 2

Leave
open

UNDERNEATH x 2

47

Miniature Dolls

MATERIALS
Thin flesh-coloured cotton knit
Stuffing wool
Fine woollen yarn for hair
Sewing thread for eyes and mouth

Miniature people are fun to play with. They can live in imaginary worlds and get up to great adventures in secret when nobody is watching! This is a simple pattern for making two differently sized dolls, an adult and a child. You can use a photocopier to enlarge or reduce the patterns as you choose. In that case, do the same with the clothes patterns.

Trace the pattern from page 52 onto paper and cut out the templates along the dotted line – in other words, without a seam allowance. Lay the pieces on doubled cotton-knit fabric. The arrows on the pattern must run in the same direction as the rib of the fabric.

Trace the pattern pieces and draw round them onto the fabric, leaving room for a seam allowance. There will be one long head, body and leg piece plus two arms for each doll.

Sew *before* you cut out the pieces! Sew using a narrow zigzag or stretch-stitch along the drawn line. Leave the top open. Cut out the pieces. Neaten the seam allowance.

Turn the pieces using a chopstick or blunt end of a barbecue stick. Make two tiny balls of stuffing wool for the feet and push them down to the bottom of the legs. Fill the legs with wool almost up to the groin (Figure 1).

Make the head and body in one, but make sure the neck is narrow. Wind a small ball from remnants of wool. Wrap a thin, even strip of wool over the ball so that both ends meet and form a backbone (Figure 2). Wrap thin strips of wool around the backbone. Wrap tightly and fasten in place occasionally with the felting needle (Figure 3). Wind the wool until the body has become almost as thick as the head. Even out using the felting needle and form the face, making it as smooth as possible (Figure 4).

Mimi and Pelle are with Auntie Anya and Uncle Anton, who have a farm. The children love to visit them. You can find their clothes on the following pages.

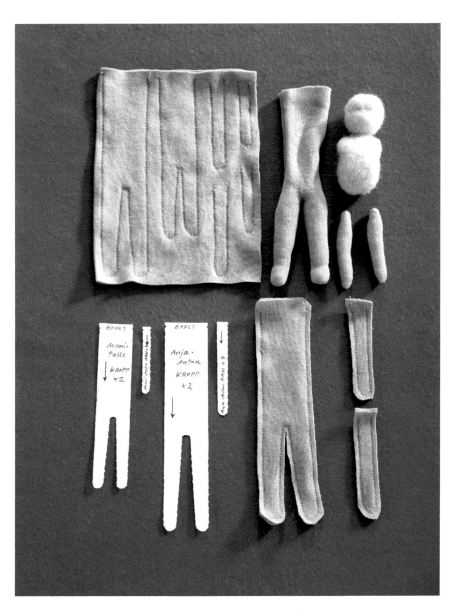

How to draw the pattern pieces onto the fabric and cut them out; stitched body; needle-felted head and body; stuffed arms.

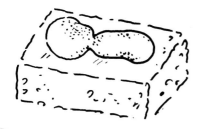

4

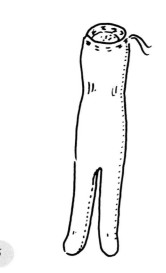

5

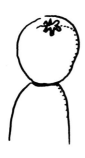

6

Pull on the body piece, bringing it up over the head. Gather together at the top by sewing running stitches around the opening (Figure 5). Wind a thread around the neck and fasten securely (Figure 6).

Fill the arms with wool up to the top (easiest using the blunt end of a barbecue skewer). Check their length (from shoulder to groin). Join at the top. Attach the arms by threading strong thread through a needle that is long enough to reach right through the body and arms. Sew several times backwards and forwards all the way through arm one, body and arm two, and fasten securely. Now the doll has moveable arms (Figure 7).

Make small stitches in sewing thread to mark the eyes and mouth, positioning them in an equilateral triangle. Children have a higher forehead than adults. The hair can be attached with sewing thread in a matching colour or with the same yarn if it is fine enough. See the hairstyles on page 53 and also those for the large doll on pages 21–24.

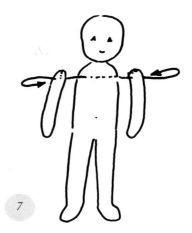

7

MINIATURE DOLLS

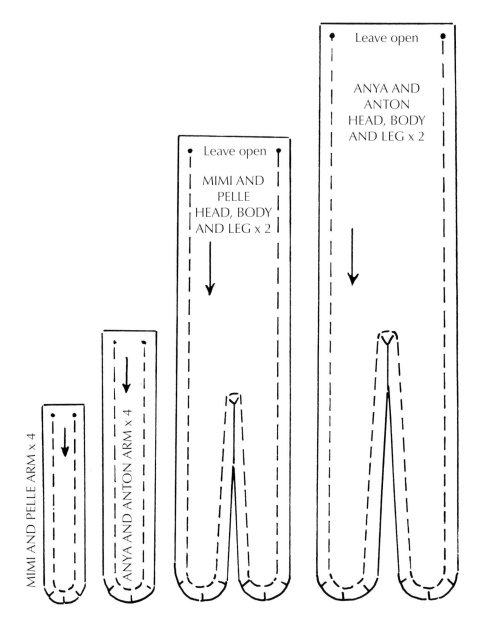

MIMI AND PELLE ARM x 4

ANYA AND ANTON ARM x 4

Leave open

MIMI AND PELLE HEAD, BODY AND LEG x 2

Leave open

ANYA AND ANTON HEAD, BODY AND LEG x 2

Hairstyles

MIMI'S HAIR

Lay long hair across the head and attach it with a centre parting. Gather the hair at the sides and sew it onto the head where the plaits will start. Make plaits. Sew the hair in place with a few stitches dotted over the head.

PELLE'S HAIR

Stitch a layer of hair to cover the scalp, either by embroidering long stitches or using parallel threads of yarn stitched into place with horizontal seams. Then stitch loops and cut through them (see also Ellie's hair p. 21–23).

ANYA'S HAIR

Undo knitted or crocheted yarn that has been moistened and allowed to dry. Make it into a tousled ball and fasten it here and there on the head using sewing thread in a matching colour (see also Kim's hair p. 22–24).

ANTON'S HAIR

Embroider long stitches close together over the head, pointing towards the middle.

TOM'S HAIR

Tom's hair is the same as Pelle's but without the loops. The fringe has been made to fall slightly to one side and left long.

SOFIA'S HAIR

Embroider as for Anton but let all the long ends come out at the back in a ponytail and sew a few strands at the front as a fringe.

HAIRSTYLES

MIMI

PELLE

ANYA · ANTON

TOM · SOFIA

Clothes for miniature dolls

Even a tiny doll needs clothes!

MATERIALS

A selection of fabrics: thin cotton, cotton jersey, silk

Cotton tape

Sewing thread in matching colours

Buttons/press studs/hook and eyelet fastenings

Thin elastic

DRESS

This dress is made from thin cotton or silk fabric, following the pattern on page 55. It is sewn in the same way as Lisa's dress, page 25.

SMALL UNDERPANTS

Measure the doll's waist. Cut a short piece of cotton tape about 2.5 cm (1 in) wide to the measured length, plus seam allowance. Fold the tape double and sew the ends with a zigzag stitch (p.55, Figure 1). Place the seam in the centre of the back and join between the legs at the base (Figure 2). Turn the pants (Figure 3). For the larger doll use wider tape.

OVERALLS

Cut 32 cm (13 in) of cotton tape 2.5 cm (1 in) wide (animal keeper Tom on page 82 has bigger overalls sewn in the same way but using 48 cm, 19 in of tape 4 cm, 1½ in wide). Cut the tape into two pieces of the same length, about 16 cm (6½ in). Measure the correct length by laying the strip over the doll's shoulder and adding a hem allowance at the bottom (p. 55, Figure 1). Turn up and hem the ends of both pieces of tape.

Fold the strips in half vertically, one length at a time, wrong side out. Sew the leg by overstitching the edges of the strips together on the inside from the hem up to the crotch (about 4 cm, 1½ in), and then on the outside from the hem up to the armhole, which could be about 1–2 cm (½–¾ in) – try it against the doll! (Figure 2)

Place both legs together and stitch the stomach and back seams from the crotch upwards, about 3.5 cm (1½ in) front and back. Make sure you leave a big enough opening for the doll to go through (Figure 3). Turn the overall right side out.

SKIRT

Cut a piece of thin cotton calico about 7 x 20 cm (2¾ x 8 in), with a piece for the lining 3 x 13 cm (1 x 5 in). For a small doll use 5 x 15 cm (2 x 6 in) and 2 x 10 cm (1¾ x 4 in) respectively.

Hem the short ends of the skirt (p. 56, Figure 1). Sew two rows of running-stitch at the top around the waist (Figure 2).

Gather the running-stitches and measure against the doll to check the skirt fits round her waist with a slight overlap. Attach the lining by sewing right sides together around the waist (Figure 3), allowing it to stick out a little at the sides. Turn under the ends of the lining (Figure 4); one of the ends can be a little longer for a button. Then fold the lining over to the wrong side where it is turned in and stitched (Figure 5).

Measure the desired length against the doll and hem the skirt (you will not have to do this if you cut out the fabric with the selvage at the bottom). Sew on a button and eyelet, or press-stud fastener.

DRESS

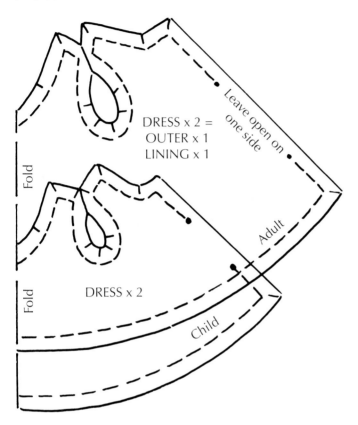

DRESS x 2 =
OUTER x 1
LINING x 1

Leave open on one side

Fold

Fold

DRESS x 2

Adult

Child

OVERALLS

1

2

3

SMALL UNDERPANTS

1

2

3

BLOUSE

Use thin cotton calico. Measure the pattern from page 57 against the doll and decide on the length. Draw the pattern onto double fabric, wrong side out. Note that the seam allowance is twice as wide over the shoulders.

Sew the shoulder seams leaving an opening at the neck (Figure 1). Fold under the seam allowance and hem around the neck. Fold in and zigzag the sleeves hem by hand (Figure 2). Fold the blouse in half, right sides facing, and stitch the sleeve and side seams (Figure 3). Hem the bottom. Thread thin elastic around the neck (Figure 4).

UNDERPANTS

Sew in thin silk or cotton knit, such as T-shirt fabric, using the pattern on page 57. Measure the doll's waist and adjust the pattern accordingly. Sew following the description for Lisa's underpants on page 25.

DUNGAREES

These trousers are sewn in the same way as Kim's dungarees on page 25, but using a much smaller pattern (see page 58). Use a thin silk or cotton fabric.

CAP

Draw the pattern from page 59 on fine leather without a seam allowance. There will be five triangular pieces, plus a peak, a strip 10 cm x 3 mm (4 x $\frac{1}{8}$ in), and a small circle 3 mm ($\frac{1}{8}$ in) in diameter.

Join two triangular pieces at a time, sewing by hand with small stitches (Figure 1), until all

SKIRT

1

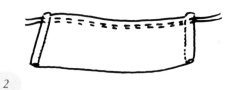

2

3

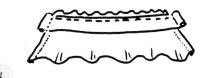

4

5

BLOUSE

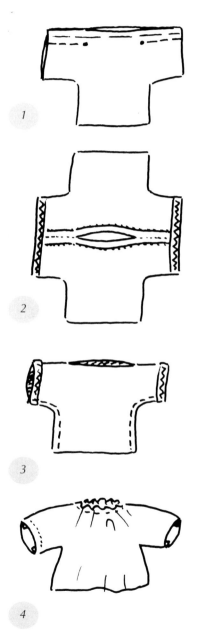

1

2

3

4

BLOUSE

BLOUSE

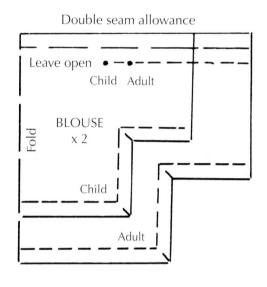

Double seam allowance

Leave open

Child   Adult

Fold

BLOUSE
x 2

Child

Adult

UNDERPANTS

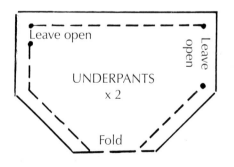

Leave open

Leave open

UNDERPANTS
x 2

Fold

five pieces have been joined. Attach the peak by sewing it to the inside (Figure 2). Glue a small strip at the bottom all around the edge and a little circle at the top (Figure 3).

JACKET

Use thin cotton or silk fabric. Try the pattern on page 59 against the doll and adjust it accordingly: it can be short or lengthened for a long coat. Draw the pattern onto fabric folded double. There will be one back piece, and two front pieces that are mirror images of each other.

Sew the back and front pieces together along the dotted line, leaving an opening to turn the jacket (Figure 1). Trim the seams and cut small notches in the seam allowance at the armholes. Turn and push out all corners using a chopstick. Sew up the openings. You can sew a decorative seam all around just inside the edges. Sew the sleeve, side and shoulder seams by hand (Figure 2). Fold down the collar, try it on the doll and sew on buttons.

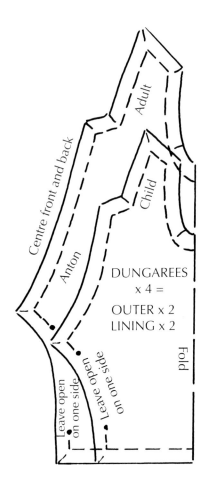

Centre front and back

Adult

Child

Anton

Leave open on one side

Leave open on one side

DUNGAREES
x 4 =

OUTER x 2
LINING x 2

Fold

CAP

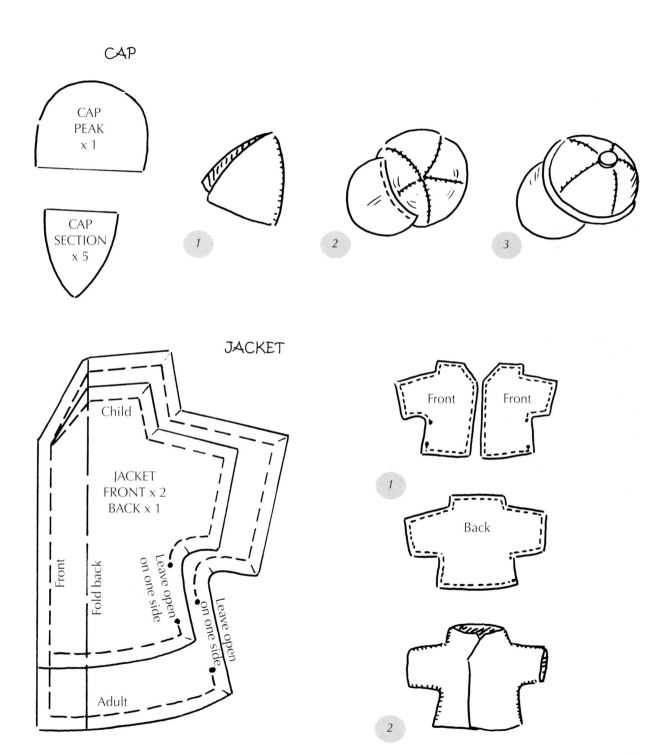

CAP
PEAK
x 1

CAP
SECTION
x 5

1

2

3

JACKET

JACKET
FRONT x 2
BACK x 1

Child

Front

Fold back

Leave open on one side

Leave open on one side

Adult

Front

Front

1

Back

2

Mimi and Pelle have taken the dogs with them for their ride in Shetland.

Farm Animals

The miniature dolls on the previous pages are designed to go with the animals in this section, so you can create a farm and let the dolls look after the animals.

Pony

MATERIALS
Thin, firm fabric such as felt
Stuffing wool
Yarn in natural fibre for mane and tail
Embroidery silk or fine yarn for eyes, nostrils
    and mouth

Trace the pattern from page 65 onto paper and cut out. Place the pieces on felt and draw round them. You should have one left-facing and one right-facing body piece, two underneath pieces, a nose and ears. Cut out the pieces.

Following the dotted line, sew the nose and ears together, right sides facing, from C to C (Figure 1). Place one body piece against the other, right sides facing. Pin and sew the neck from A to B (Figure 2). Pin and stitch on the nose/ears by hand, between the cheeks, from A up to C and on to D on both sides (Figure 3).

Prepare the mane by winding the yarn around 2 or 3 fingers. Pull it off carefully. Prepare the tail by winding yarn around all your fingers but not as many times as for the mane. Pull it off your fingers, tie one end together, winding a few times around the top, and attach it securely (Figure 4).

Insert the mane between the body pieces from D to E, leaving a little sticking out between the fabric (Figure 5). Sew the mane in place at the same time as you stitch along the upper neck,

from D to E. Insert the whole tail between the body pieces so just a small amount of the bound end protrudes. Sew from E to F, fixing the tail in place (Figure 5).

Place the two underneath pieces together, right sides facing, and sew them from B to F, leaving the middle third open for turning (Figure 6). Position the joined underneath section against the body's splayed legs, right sides facing. Sew from B round one front leg, along the stomach, round a back leg and up to F. Do the same on the other side (Figure 7). Turn the horse right side out through the gap in the stomach.

Cut open the mane and tail loops and trim to the desired length. Stuff the horse (apart from the ears) using washed and carded stuffing wool. Use a bamboo chopstick to insert the wool properly. Stuff firmly so the pony is stable enough to be ridden.

Form the legs from tightly bound wool (using the same method as for the doll, p. 18), making them longer than the fabric legs and holding the wool in place with the felting needle (Figure 8). When the wool legs have been inserted, fill around them and under the stomach with stuffing so that the legs stay firmly in position (Figure 8). Close the stomach opening with slip-stitch.

Add a few extra lengths of yarn to the mane by sewing them at right angles over the neck and allowing a few strands to fall forwards between the ears as a fringe. Attach with sewing thread in a similar colour. Sew eyes and nostrils in fine brown yarn, and add a bridle from brown yarn if you like.

Spaniel

MATERIALS
Thin velvet, flannel or felt in brown and white
Stuffing wool
Black yarn or buttonhole silk for nose and eyes

Trace the pattern from page 65 onto paper, cut out and draw round the pieces on the wrong side of the fabric. You should have two brown body halves – one right-facing and one left-facing, right and left pieces for the tail, one ear piece, and left and right underneath sections in white. Cut out the pieces.

Put the tail pieces together, right sides facing, and sew (Figure 1). Turn the tail. Place the body sides together, right sides facing, pin and sew from A to B. Pin the back from C to D, insert the tail (turned right side out) and sew along the back, from C to D (Figure 2).

Pin the ears in place and sew by hand from A to C on each side (Figure 3). Lay the underneath pieces on top of each other, right sides facing. Sew along the stomach from B to D, leaving the middle third open for turning (Figure 4).

Bend back the legs on each side of the body and place the underneath section onto the body with the legs placed on top of each other, right sides facing. Pin and sew around the legs, two seams from B to D (Figure 5). Trim the seams, cutting small notches in the seam allowance, and turn right side out. Stuff the dog and stitch the opening.

Sew eyes and nose with black yarn or buttonhole silk. Attach the front edge of the ears to the cheek with invisible slip-stitches.

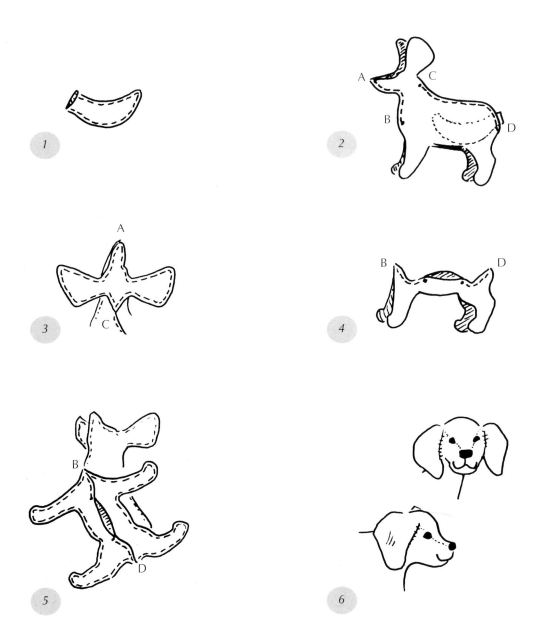

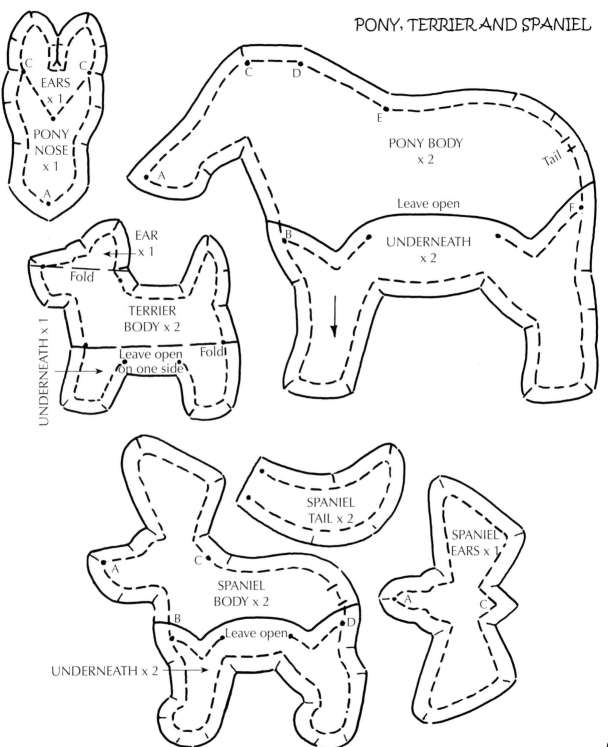

PONY, TERRIER AND SPANIEL

EARS
x 1

C   C

PONY
NOSE
x 1

A

PONY BODY
x 2

C   D

E

Tail

A

Leave open

B

UNDERNEATH
x 2

F

EAR
x 1

Fold

TERRIER
BODY x 2

UNDERNEATH x 1

Leave open
on one side

Fold

SPANIEL
TAIL x 2

SPANIEL
EARS x 1

A   C

SPANIEL
BODY x 2

B

Leave open

D

A   C

UNDERNEATH x 2

Terrier

MATERIALS

White or black hobby felt or other thin fabric
(white for a West Highland terrier, black for a
Scottish terrier); you can use fur fabric for a
larger version

Stuffing wool

Black or brown yarn for nose and eyes

Trace the pattern from page 65 and cut out the
pieces. Allow room for seam allowances when
you position the templates on the fabric. There
will be one left-hand and one right-hand body
piece, an underneath piece (centre fold at the
stomach) and an ear piece (centre fold between
the ears). Cut out the pieces.

Lay the body halves together, right sides facing,
and sew from A to B (Figure 1). Insert the ear piece,
right sides facing, and sew it in place along the
sides and around the ears from A to C (Figure 2).

Bend the legs apart and insert the underneath
section, sewing it with right sides facing around
all four legs, leaving an opening on one side of
the stomach to allow for turning (Figure 3). Turn
and stuff with wool and sew up the stomach
opening. Sew on eyes and a nose.

*Terrier, larger than actual size,
sewn in cuddly wool fur fabric.*

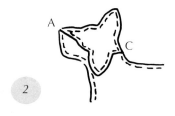

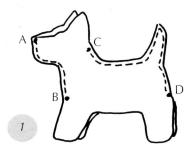

Cow

MATERIALS

Stiff woollen or cotton fabric in a suitable cow
colour (white cotton or rough dupioni silk
can be painted with textile pens to make a
spotted cow)

Small piece of silk fabric in a different colour for
horns

Stuffing wool

Fine woollen yarn for tail, attaching horns and
sewing eyes and nostrils

Thin pink cotton fabric for udder

Trace the pattern pieces from page 70 onto paper,
cut them out and draw round them on the wrong
side of the fabric. You will have one left and
one right side each for the body, two head and
underneath pieces, plus a head gusset. Use the
pink fabric for two udder sides. Cut out the pieces.

Twist some yarn to make a thin tail with a tassel
at the tip.

Place the head pieces, right sides facing, onto
the body pieces. Pin, tack and sew from A round
the ear to B (p. 68, Figure 1).

Put one body piece on top of the other, right
sides facing, pin and sew from C to D (Figure 2).
Insert the tail between the body sides so that the
tail is inside with just a small end sticking out
from the fabric. Pin and sew the back seam from
E to F, stitching the tail in place at the same time
(Figure 2).

Pin and sew the head gusset so that C matches
C on the nose and E matches E on the neck
(Figure 3).

Place one underneath section on top of the
other, right sides facing, pin and sew the stomach
seam from D to F, leaving the middle third open
for turning (Figure 4). Fold up the legs on one
side of the body, lay the underneath piece against
the legs, right sides facing, and pin. Sew from D
to F around the legs on both sides (Figure 5).

Cut small notches in the seam allowance at all
corners and turn. Stuff the cow well, especially in
and above the legs so that it stands firmly (if you
like, make wool legs following the instructions
for the pony on p. 62). Do not stuff the ears. Sew
up the stomach opening.

Place the udder pieces together, right sides facing, and sew the sides (Figure 6). Open out the teats, fold the edge in slightly and sew together by hand (Figure 7). Trim then turn the udder. Fill it with a tuft of wool and attach it by hand between and slightly in front of the back legs of the cow.

Draw around the horn pattern onto thin fabric, sew round and trim, then stuff the horns with a little wool using a chopstick. Sew the opening. Attach the horns on top of the head with large stitches (Figure 8).

Embroider on the eyes and nostrils.

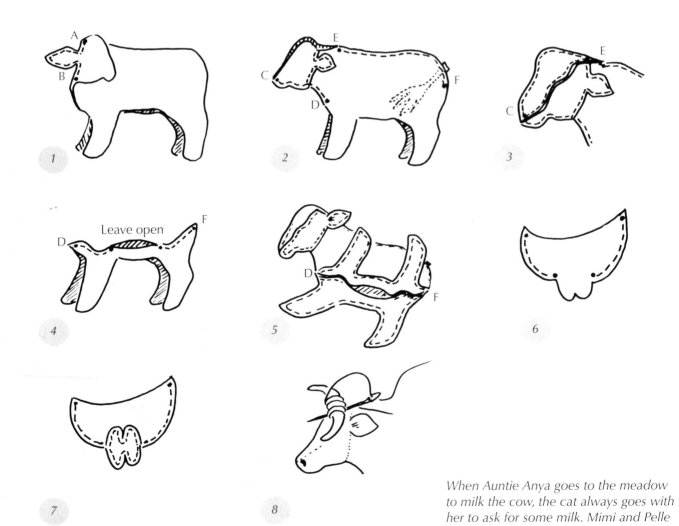

When Auntie Anya goes to the meadow to milk the cow, the cat always goes with her to ask for some milk. Mimi and Pelle want to try milking too.

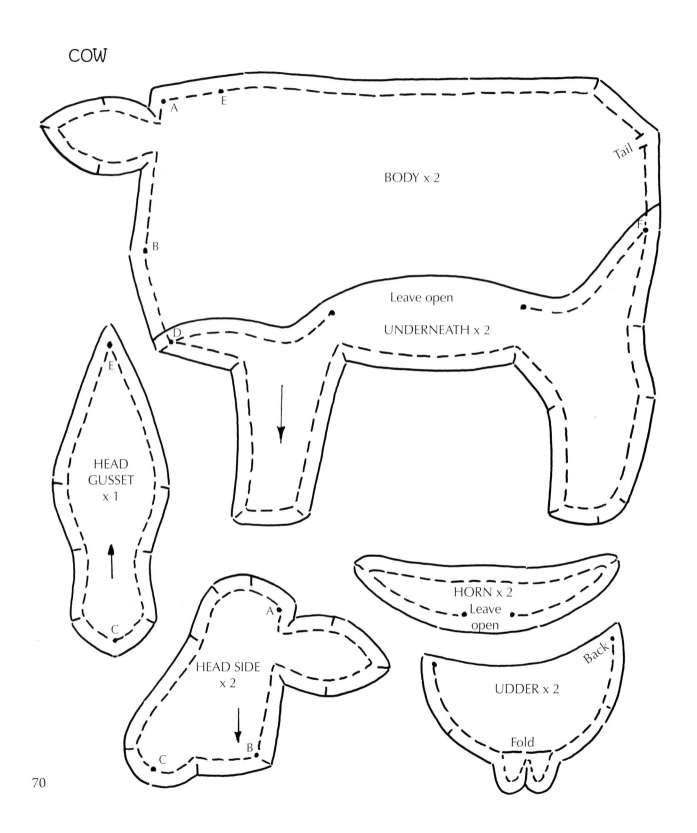

COW

BODY x 2

Tail

A E

B

HEAD
GUSSET
x 1

E

C

Leave open

UNDERNEATH x 2

D

F

HEAD SIDE
x 2

A

C B

HORN x 2
Leave
open

Back

UDDER x 2

Fold

70

Sheep

MATERIALS
Small piece of grey, white or black hobby felt
2 pipe-cleaners, 16 cm (6¼ in) long
Unspun wool for wrapping (such as grey, white or black magic wool)

Place the sheep's head pattern (p. 74) onto felt folded double. Draw round and sew following the dotted line (Figure 1). Cut out and turn. Stuff the head with a little wool. Cut out two ears of felt, following the pattern on page 74, pinch them together at the base and attach them to the sides of the head so that they stick out sideways (Figure 2). Cut two strips of felt 3 x 14 cm (1 x 5½ in).

Take one pipe-cleaner, fold it in at each end so that it's slightly shorter than the strip of felt, and do the same with the other one (Figure 3). Lay one pipe-cleaner on a strip of felt, making sure the felt is a little longer than the pipe-cleaner. Fold in the long sides of the felt and sew a third of the way in from each end (these end bits will be legs). Insert the pipe-cleaner into the felt and bend the covered leg parts at right angles to the uncovered body (Figure 3). Do the same with the other pipe-cleaner.

Using a few big stitches fasten the body part of each pipe-cleaner together. Sew the neck to the body (Figure 4). Take wide thin tufts of wool and wrap around the sheep's body in different directions, wrapping once between the legs (Figure 5). Wrap until the sheep is fat (Figure 6).

If you are making several sheep you can attach the heads differently for each one, and angle the ears differently too.

LAMB

The lamb is made in the same way as the sheep but in a smaller size. Use the smaller head and ear templates (p. 74). Cut two pieces of pipe-cleaner 12 cm (4¾ in) long and bend in each end to make them just under 10 cm (4 in) long. The two felt pieces required measure 2.5 x 10 cm (¾ x 4 in).

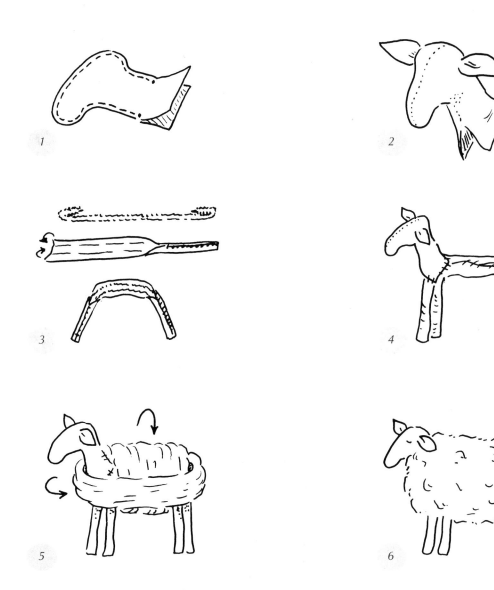

As soon as Anton takes his bucket of food to the sheep, they come rushing up and gather around him, bleating.

PIG/SHEEP

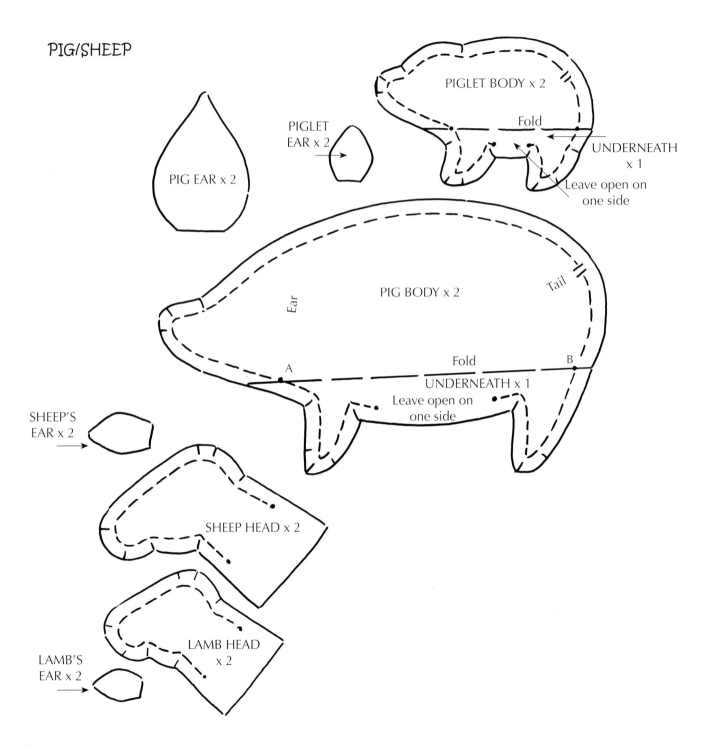

PIG EAR x 2

PIGLET
EAR x 2

PIGLET BODY x 2

Fold

UNDERNEATH
x 1

Leave open on
one side

Ear

PIG BODY x 2

Tail

A

Fold

B

UNDERNEATH x 1

Leave open on
one side

SHEEP'S
EAR x 2

SHEEP HEAD x 2

LAMB HEAD
x 2

LAMB'S
EAR x 2

Pig and piglet

MATERIALS
Pink felt or flannel
Stuffing wool
Pink yarn for the tail
Pink sewing thread

Trace or copy the pattern from page 74 onto paper. Cut the pieces out and draw round them onto the fabric. You will have one left and one right body piece, an underneath piece, plus two ears for each pig. Mark A and B on the body pieces.

Cut a small piece of pink wool about 5 cm (2 in) long for the sow and shorter for the piglets.

Place the body pieces together, inserting the tail between them so a little bit sticks out. Pin and sew from A around the snout, along the back and over the tail to B (Figure 1).

Bend the legs apart, place the underneath section against them, right sides facing, pin and sew around all four legs, leaving the seam open on one side of the stomach to allow for turning (Figure 2). Cut small notches in the seam allowance at the corners of the legs. Turn and stuff the pig, making it really round. The piglets can be a bit thinner. Stitch the opening.

If using felt, the ears are ready to attach: pinch the base together (Figure 3) and sew them onto the head, facing forwards. If using a fabric that frays, zigzag around the ear first.

Pig's eyes are small so make dots with a pencil or sew a tiny stitch. Make an indentation in the snout.

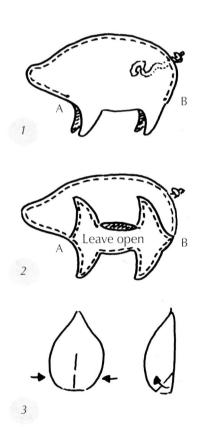

Hen and cockerel

MATERIALS
10 cm (4 in) tubular gauze bandage, about 4 cm
    (1½ in) wide
Stuffing wool
Red and yellow yarn
Embroidery needle
White sewing thread

Twist the tubular gauze bandage once in the middle (Figure 1) and thread one half over the other to make a little bag. Insert a small amount of wool (Figure 2). Sew a few stitches right through the body at the back to make a feathered tail (Figure 3).

Run gathering stitches around the neck and sew a few stitches here and there to give the desired shape. Using red yarn, embroider a small comb on top of the head and a wattle under the chin (Figure 4). Use yellow yarn to sew a loop for the beak by sticking the needle into the body and bringing it out between the comb and the wattle. Turn back on the same spot and bring the yarn out through the body again. Mark small dots for eyes (Figure 4).

Make several hens – they don't like being alone! Make the cockerel a little larger than the others (Figure 5). You can sew the hens to a branch or put them in a nest.

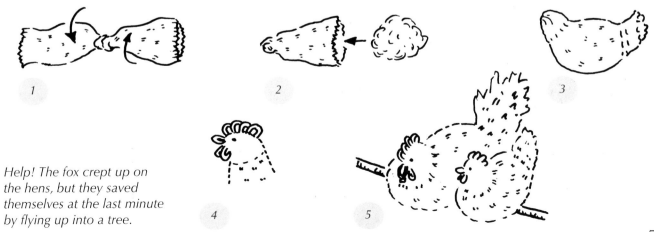

1

2

3

Help! The fox crept up on the hens, but they saved themselves at the last minute by flying up into a tree.

4

5

Wildlife Park

These animals are also designed to match the size of the small dolls in this book. You can make enclosures for the animals from small twigs or bricks.

Bear

MATERIALS
Fur fabric, brown woollen fabric, towelling or
    velvet
Stuffing wool
Brown or black yarn for eyes and nose

Trace or copy the pattern from page 80 onto paper and cut out. Draw round the pattern onto the wrong side of the fabric. You will have one back and two sides. Cut out the pieces.

Place the side pieces, right sides facing, and sew from A to B (Figure 1). Lay the sides onto the back piece, right sides facing. Pin and sew from C round the ear, the arm and the leg to D. Repeat on the other side (Figure 2).

Fold down the nose gusset and sew it to the sides from C to A. Trim and then cut small notches in the seam allowance as indicated on the pattern. Turn. Sew a couple of stitches at the base of each ear so they will not be filled when the bear is stuffed.

Stuff the head firmly with wool, adding a small hard ball of wool for the nose at the tip. Stuff the arms, legs and body fairly loosely so that the bear can change its position. Sew the stomach opening with ladder-stitch (see page 12). Sew on the eyes and nose.

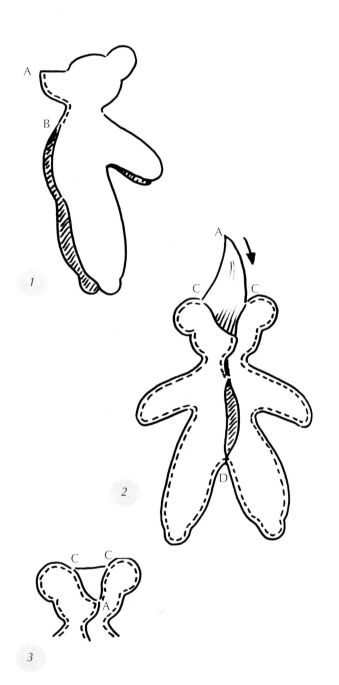

Sophie has taken the children to the wildlife park today. First they go and watch the bear cubs playing.

BEAR

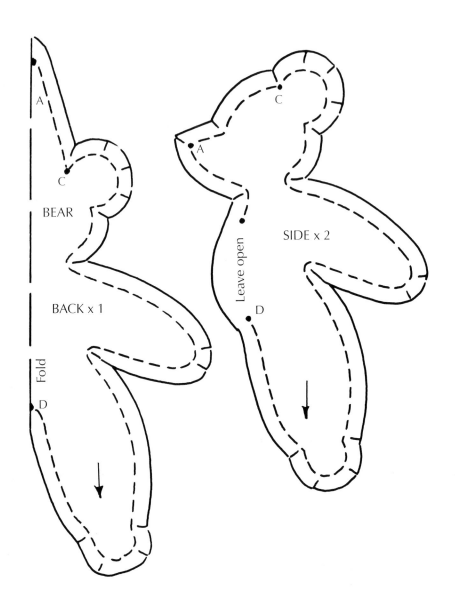

BEAR

C

BACK x 1

Fold

D

A

C

SIDE x 2

Leave open

D

Elk

MATERIALS

Firm dark-brown fabric, fluffy if possible
Stuffing wool
Small piece of beige silk for horns
Black thread for eyes and nostrils
A pipe-cleaner

Trace the pattern from page 84 onto paper and cut out. Position and draw round the pieces on the wrong side of the fabric so that you have one left and one right side, two underneath sections and a head gusset, plus two antlers. Cut out the pieces.

Lay the body halves together, right sides facing. Pin and sew from A to B under the chin and from C to D along the back (Figure 1). Tack then sew on the head gusset, right sides facing, from A and over the ear to C on both sides (Figure 2).

Place the underneath sections together, right sides facing. Pin and sew the stomach seam from B to D, leaving the middle third open to allow for turning (Figure 3). Lay the joined underneath section on the body's legs, right sides facing, and sew from B to D around the legs on one side. Repeat on the other side (Figure 4). Trim and then cut small notches in the seam allowance as shown on the pattern (p. 84) and turn right side out.

Sew a few stitches at the base of the ears to prevent wool getting in when you stuff the head (Figure 5). Stuff the head but not the ears. Stuff the legs firmly and fill the entire body. Sew the

stomach opening together. Sew a row of gathering stitches around the muzzle (Figure 6). Stitch on eyes and nostrils using black thread.

Make the antlers from golden-brown fabric, preferably dupioni silk. Trim carefully and cut small notches in the seam allowance between all the antler horns. Turn the antlers using the blunt end of a barbecue skewer. Insert a curved piece of pipe-cleaner into the centre part of the antlers (Figure 7). Attach the antlers by sewing them in front of the ears with yarn the same colour as the body fabric.

If the elk's legs bend outwards you can sew large stitches between the legs at the top to keep them together.

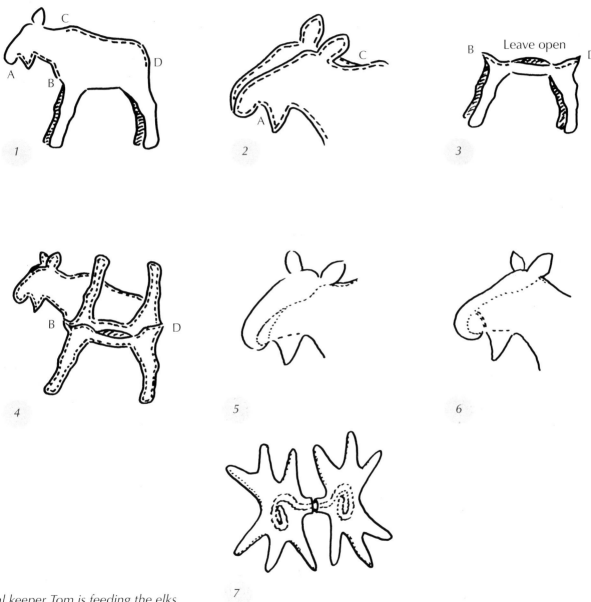

1

2

C

3

B   Leave open   D

4

B   D

5

6

7

Animal keeper Tom is feeding the elks with apples and Pelle has climbed up on the fence to see better.

83

ELK

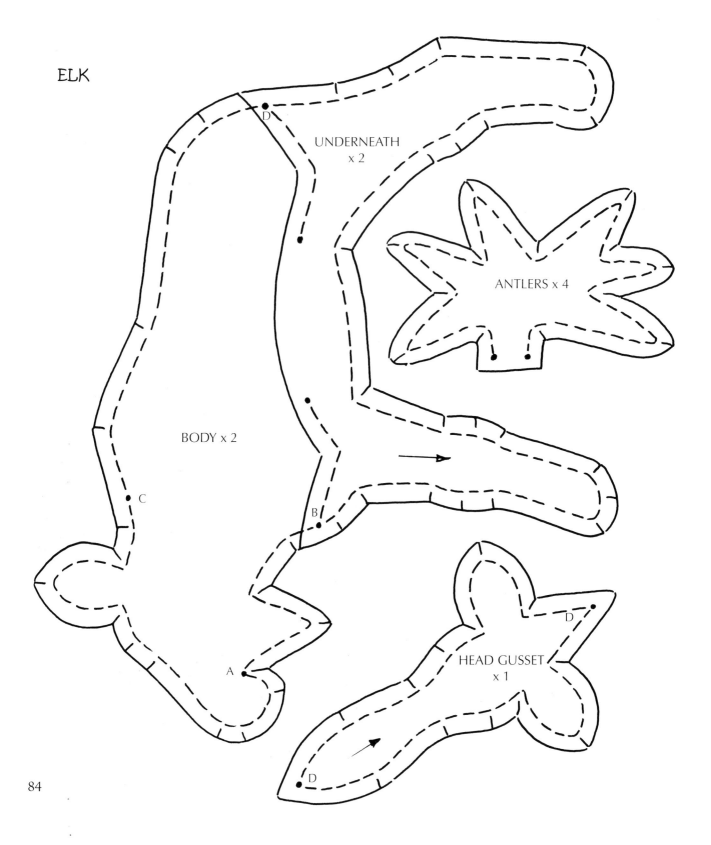

UNDERNEATH
x 2

ANTLERS x 4

BODY x 2

C

B

A

HEAD GUSSET
x 1

D

D

D

84

TURTLE

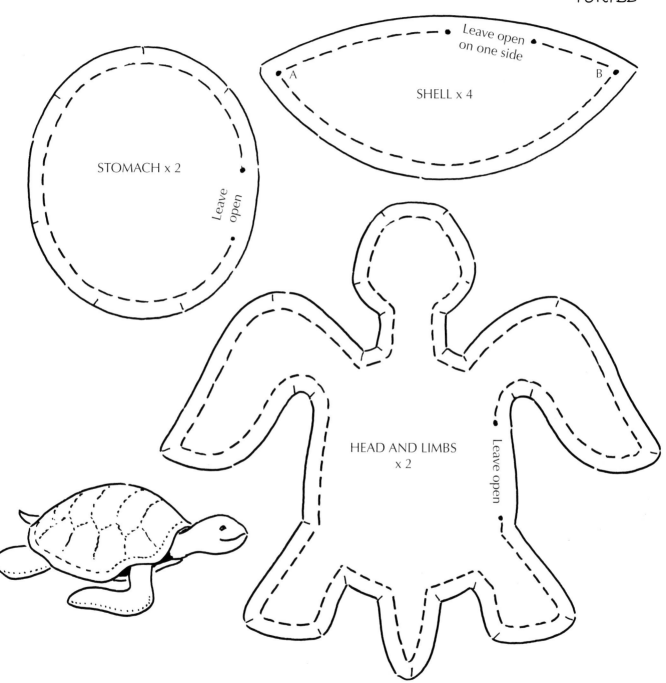

STOMACH x 2

Leave open

SHELL x 4

Leave open on one side

A

B

HEAD AND LIMBS x 2

Leave open

Inside the aquarium it's exciting to look at the sharks and turtles swimming so gracefully behind the glass. You can find Sophia's red jacket on page 58.

Turtle

MATERIALS

Silk, taffeta or other fine fabric in dark green and
    yellow
Stuffing wool
Sewing thread in dark green for shell, yellow or
    white for eyes

Trace the pattern from page 85 onto paper and
cut out. Draw round the pieces onto fabric.
There will be four green shell pieces, two yellow
stomach pieces and two green head-limb pieces.

Lay the shell halves two and two, right sides
facing, and sew both pairs from A to B along
the straighter sides. Leave an opening on one of
them to allow for turning (Figure 1). Open out the
halves, place them together right sides facing and
sew around all the outside edge (Figure 2). Turn
the shell and sew lines to make a pattern and
around the inside edge (Figure 3).

Place the yellow stomach pieces together and
sew round them, leaving an opening for turning.
Turn and sew up the opening.

Place the head and limb pieces together and
sew all around, leaving an opening (Figure 4).
Turn (with the help of a skewer) and stuff the head
until it is round and firm. Stuff the legs and tail
using slightly less wool. Sew up the opening.

Pin the shell on top and the yellow stomach
underneath and sew them securely together.
Leave an opening and fill with wool under
the shell until it is nicely rounded. Sew up the
opening. Stitch eyes and possibly a mouth with
sewing thread.

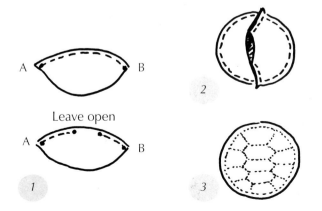

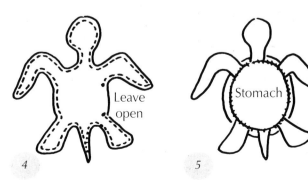

Shark

MATERIALS

Dupioni silk, taffeta lining or thin cotton fabric
  in grey and white
Stuffing wool
Textile pen or embroidery thread

Copy the pattern from page 89. Draw round the
paper pattern pieces onto the wrong side of the
fabric. There will be one left and one right side
in grey and a stomach in white. Place the side
pieces together, right sides facing, pin and sew
from A on the nose, around the back fin and
along to the tail fin at B (Figure 1).

Open out the side pieces and place the
stomach piece against them, right sides facing.
Pin and sew around the whole stomach piece but
leave an opening on one side to allow for turning
(Figure 2). Trim the seams and cut small notches
at all sharp angles along the seam allowance.

Turn right side out, making sure the fins are
pushed out completely.

Sew a seam along the base of the fin on the
back (the fins will not be stuffed with wool). Stuff
the shark and sew up the opening.

Draw or embroider a mouth with a zigzag line
for the teeth. Make dots for the eyes (Figure 3).

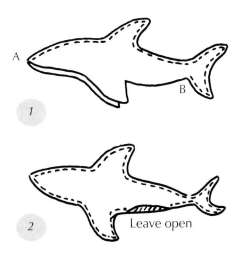

A

B

1

2 Leave open

3

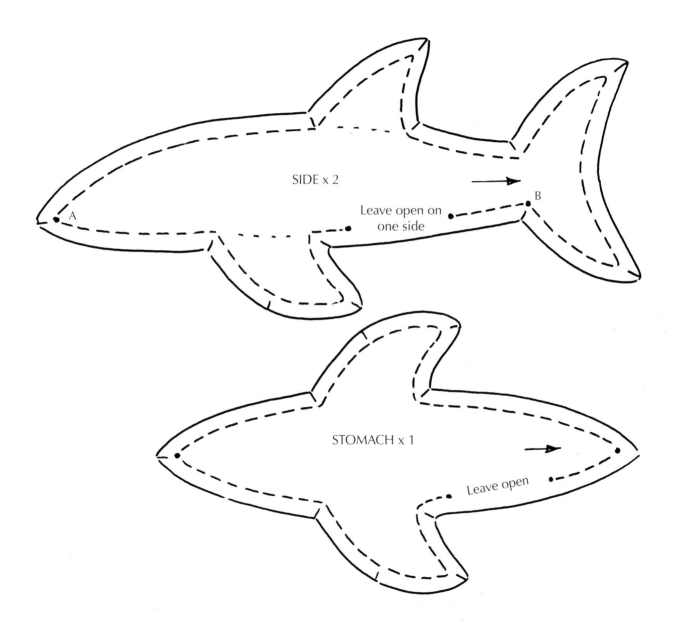

SIDE x 2

A

B

Leave open on
one side

STOMACH x 1

Leave open

Rhinoceros

MATERIALS
Dark-grey raw silk, taffeta lining or cotton fabric
Stuffing wool
Yarn for tail
Embroidery thread or textile pen for armour and facial features

Trace the pattern from page 92 onto paper and cut it out. Draw around the pieces onto the wrong side of the fabric so that you have one left and one right body section, one left and one right underneath section, and four ear pieces. Cut out the pieces.

Sew the ears together and turn. Make a fold at the base and sew the ears together making sure they are the same length (p. 93, Figure 1).

Wind a little yarn around three fingers, pull it off, then wrap and fasten yarn around half of its length, making a tail with a tassel at the end. Cut through the yarn loops.

Place the body pieces together, right sides facing. Pin and sew from A around the horn, inserting the ears between the body pieces so that only the base of the ears protrudes. Sew them in place and continue sewing along the back. Insert the tail with the tassel inside the fabric, sew it in place and finish at B (Figure 2).

Place the underneath sections together, right sides facing, and sew from A to B, leaving the middle third open to allow for turning (Figure 3).

Open out the legs and lay the underneath section against them. Pin and sew the legs together, one side at a time, from A to B (Figure 4). Trim the seam and cut small notches in all sharp angles.

Turn and stuff using a chopstick to help. Make woollen legs that are a couple of centimetres longer than the leg fabric (the same technique as for the doll's arms and legs, p. 18–19). Stuff the head and horn carefully, insert the wool legs into the fabric and add extra stuffing between the upper ends of the wool legs. Stuff the body firmly.

Sew up the stomach opening. Draw or embroider eyes and nostrils. Embroider a line in chain stitch (Figure 5), or draw using a textile pen, across the back and down the sides as in the photo on page 90.

The rhinoceros and the elephant
share this wonderful grassy jungle!

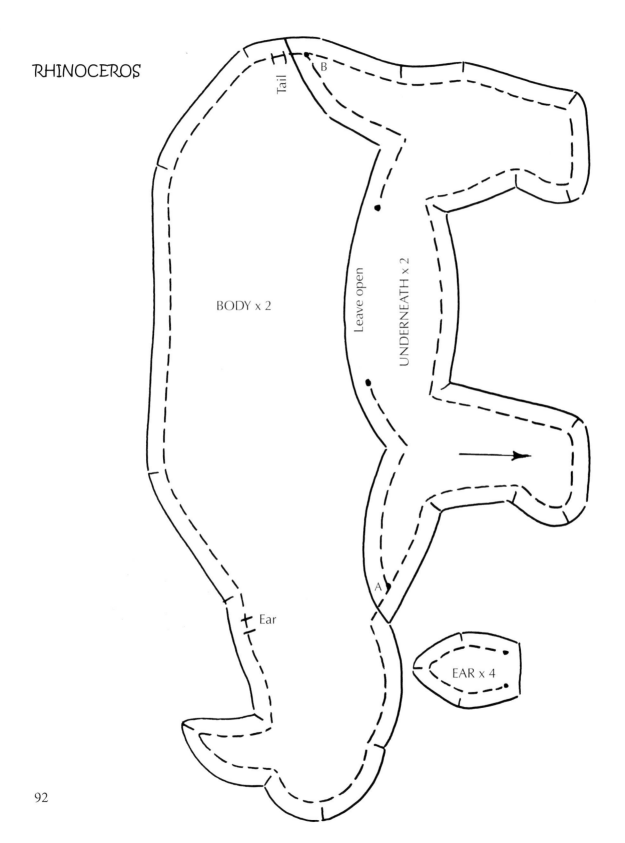

RHINOCEROS

BODY x 2

Tail

B

Leave open

UNDERNEATH x 2

A

Ear

EAR x 4

92

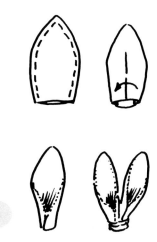

1

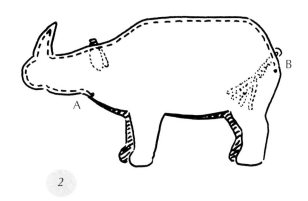

2

3

4

Chain stitch

5

Elephant

Firm grey fabric in natural fibre, preferably
   velvet or felt
Stuffing wool
Shiny black thread or small black beads for eyes
Thin rolls of white felt for tusks
Rolled-up fabric or small yarn tassel for tail

Trace or copy the pattern templates from page 95
onto paper and cut them out. Draw round them
on the wrong side of the fabric. You need one left-
facing and one right-facing body piece, a left and
right underneath piece, and two left and two right
ear pieces. Mark the dots on the seam allowance.
Cut out the pieces.

Place the body pieces together, right sides
facing. Pin and sew following the dotted line
from A to B around the trunk and along the back
(Figure 1). Leave an opening between B and C.

Place the underneath sections together, right
sides facing, and pin and sew them together from
A to C (Figure 2).

Fold up the legs on one side towards the body
then pin and sew the legs of the underneath
section to the legs of the body piece. Do the same
on the other side (Figure 3). Make small cuts in
the seam allowance under the chin and between
the legs to make turning easier.

Turn through the opening B to C and stuff the
whole elephant with the help of a chopstick.
You can use rolls of old blanket fabric to fill the
legs to make the elephant extra stable. Make
the rolls a couple of centimetres longer than the

legs. Otherwise make woollen legs following the
instructions for the pony on page 62.

Make small indentations at the end of the
stuffed trunk to resemble nostrils.

Cut one end of the tail piece to make a fringe.
Roll the tail piece lengthwise and stitch it together
with slip-stitch (Figure 4). The tail can also be
made from a piece of yarn. Attach the tail at the
same time as the rear opening is sewn together.

Place the ear pieces right sides facing and sew
round, leaving an opening for turning (Figure
5). Turn and sew up the opening. Do not stuff
the ears. African elephants have big ears; Indian
elephants' ears are smaller (and Indian elephants
are easier to tame). Attach the ears. Check from
above to make sure they are both the same
distance from the forehead.

Sew on the eyes using small stitches or make
them from two small black beads (Figure 6).

ELEPHANT

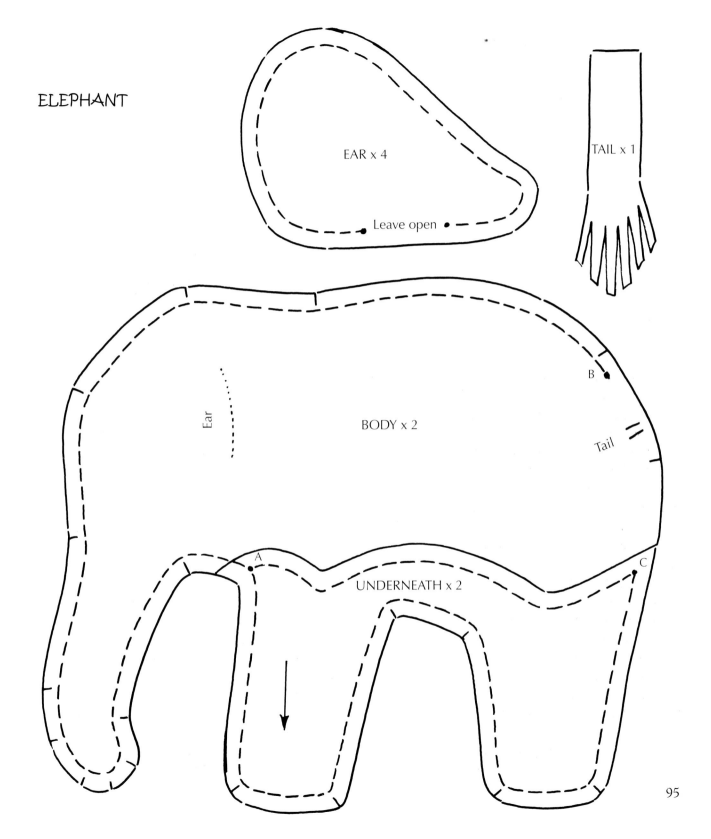

EAR x 4

Leave open

TAIL x 1

B

Ear

BODY x 2

Tail

A

UNDERNEATH x 2

C

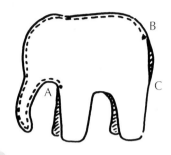

1

2

3

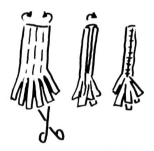

4

5

6

Penguin

MATERIALS
Black and white hobby felt
Stuffing wool
Red thread for beak
White and black sewing thread

Copy or trace the pattern templates from page 98 onto paper and cut them out. Draw round them onto felt. You will need one left-facing and one right-facing side in black felt, plus a front piece and a round base piece in white felt. Cut out the pieces. Lay the side pieces together and pin and sew from A under the beak and along the back to B (Figure 1).

Fold out the wings and position the stomach piece so that the white wings match the body's black wings. Pin and sew from A to C on each side (Figure 2).

Trim the seams, especially around the wing tips, and make small cuts in the angles beneath them. Turn and stuff the head and body but not the wings. Sew the base section in place with the seam allowance facing outwards (Figure 3).

Mark a beak with a few red stitches. Sew round, white eyes with a black dot in the middle.

PENGUIN

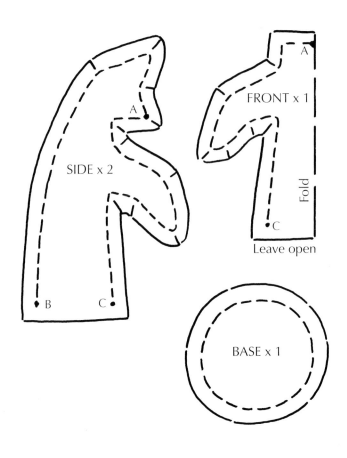

SIDE x 2

FRONT x 1

Fold

Leave open

A

B

C

BASE x 1

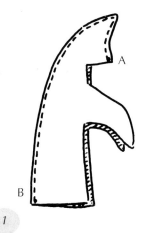

A

B

1

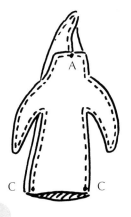

A

C   C

2

3

Seal and pup

MATERIALS
Thin grey fabric, preferably silk (dupioni, Thai)
   or taffeta
Stuffing wool
Fine grey or dark-brown yarn for eyes and nose
Sewing thread for whiskers

Trace the pattern pieces from page 101 onto thin paper or copy them. Cut them out. Draw onto the material one left-facing and one right-facing side, two underneath sections and a head gusset. Mark the dots on the seam allowance. Cut out the pieces.

Place the side pieces together, right sides facing. Pin them and sew from A to B and from C to D (p. 101, Figure 1). Tack the head gusset in place and sew it (Figure 2). Take care sewing the curve around the nose.

Place the underneath pieces together, right sides facing. Pin and sew the stomach seam, leaving a gap in the middle for turning (Figure 3). Fold up one front flipper and stomach towards the side. Spread out the underneath section and place it, right sides facing, against the body piece. Pin and sew the front flipper, stomach and back flipper from B to D, and then do the same on the other side (Figure 4).

Turn right side out and stuff the head and nose firmly, then the body. Stuff the flippers with a little wool or leave unfilled. Sew up the stomach opening.

Sew or draw large round eyes, place them on or immediately outside the gusset seams. The nose can be marked with two stitches for nostrils. Make whiskers if you like, using sewing thread (Figure 5).

*The seals and penguins are sunning themselves
on a rock in the middle of their large pool.*

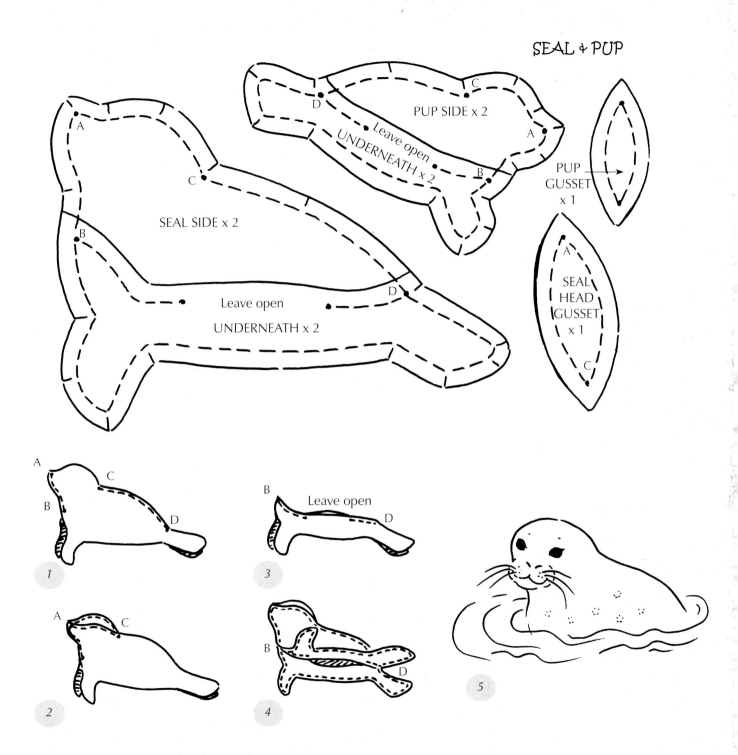

SEAL & PUP

PUP SIDE x 2

Leave open
UNDERNEATH x 2

A

C

SEAL SIDE x 2

B

Leave open

D

UNDERNEATH x 2

PUP
GUSSET
x 1

A

SEAL
HEAD
GUSSET
x 1

C

A
C
B
D

1

B   Leave open
D

3

A   C

2

B
D

4

5

Glove Puppets

You will have lots of fun with children as soon as you put one of these glove puppets on your hand and start talking or telling a story. Here are the instructions for the *Red Riding Hood* characters:

Red Riding Hood, Grandma and Huntsman

MATERIALS
Flesh-coloured cotton knit
Velour or cotton knit for the outfits (red, white, green)
Yarn or wool for hair
Stuffing wool
Textile pen or embroidery thread for eyes and mouth

Cut out the patterns on pages 104 and 105 in paper, and transfer them to the fabric. Sew the fabric pieces – before you cut them out – using stretch-stitch following the dotted lines.

Draw, pin and sew two hands from flesh-coloured cotton knit folded double.

Draw, pin and sew the head (p. 105, Figure 1) from four layers of flesh-coloured cotton knit.

Draw, pin and sew the bodies from velour folded double (wrong side out). Leave openings for hands and at the bottom (Figure 2).

Cut out the head and hands and turn right side out. Cut out the body. Stuff the hands with wool. Sew a row of running stitches around the sleeve opening, insert one hand, pull the gathering tight and attach the hand securely by stitching backwards and forwards through the sleeves and wrist (Figure 3). Repeat for the other hand.

Turn the body. Stuff wool into the head's two outer pockets, leaving the middle pocket empty. Stuff as evenly as you can so the head is nicely rounded. Close the outer pockets using back-stitch around the throat so that the wool stays in the head and does not slip down into the neck. Push the neck of the body piece as far as you can into the head, using your index finger to help, and sew the head's neck in place onto the body (Figure 4), using strong thread and winding several times around the neck.

Hem the bottom edge. Sew or draw eyes and mouth. Sew on hair (follow the hairstyles on page 21–24). Hair made of grey wool would be ideal for Grandma. Make a hood from a piece of red fabric by measuring the circumference of the head and making that the hood's long side. Sew together to form a tube, gather one end and stitch the hood to the hair with a small hem turned inwards.

The tale of Red Riding Hood and the wolf works especially well with glove puppets.

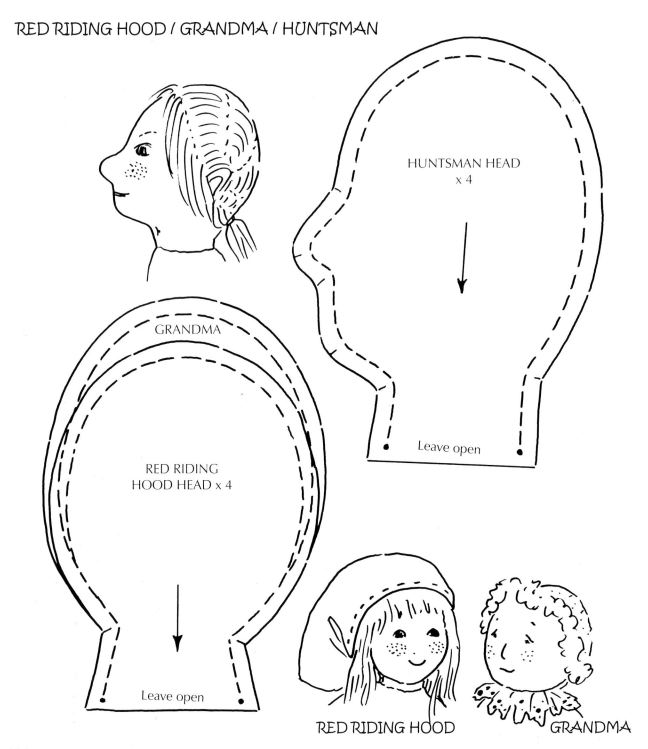

HUNTSMAN HEAD
x 4

Leave open

GRANDMA

RED RIDING
HOOD HEAD x 4

Leave open

RED RIDING HOOD

GRANDMA

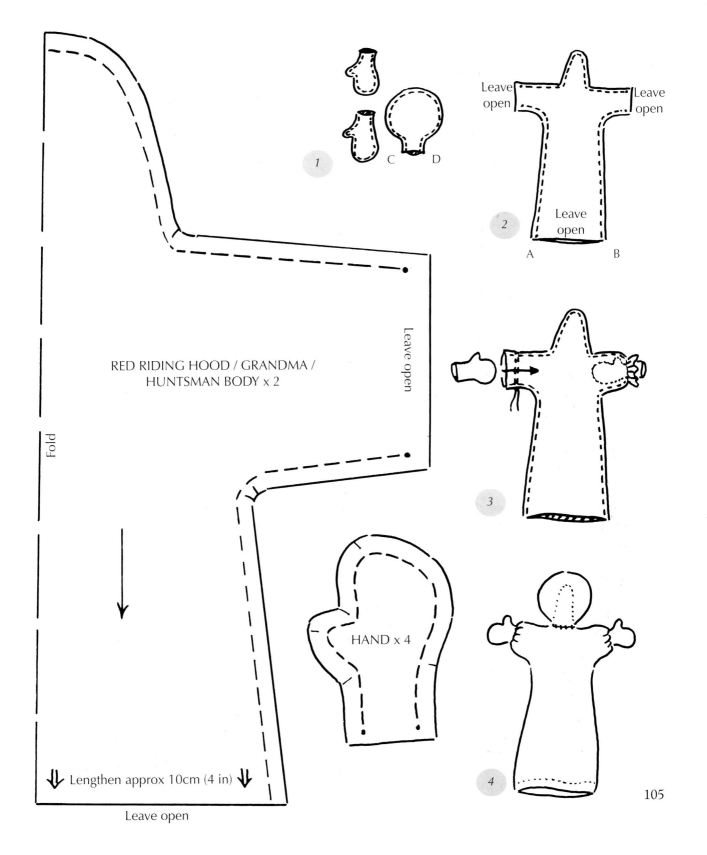

Fold

RED RIDING HOOD / GRANDMA /
HUNTSMAN BODY x 2

Leave open

Lengthen approx 10cm (4 in)

Leave open

1

C   D

Leave
open

Leave
open

Leave
open

2

A   B

3

HAND x 4

4

105

Wolf

MATERIALS
Grey fur, woollen fabric or towelling
Red cotton or silk fabric for mouth and tongue
Stuffing wool
A small piece of yellow felt for eyes
Black yarn for pupils and nose, grey for claws

Draw round the pattern pieces on the wrong side of the fabric, bearing in mind the direction of the fur's pile (follow the arrows on the pattern, p. 108). In grey you will have: two bodies, one face, one back of head and one chin/throat piece. In red: two tongues and two mouth halves (p. 107, Figure 1).

Cut out the pieces. Lay the body pieces together, right sides facing, and sew from A to B, all the way round the arm and paw (Figure 2). Leave the neck and the bottom of the body open. Hem or zigzag the lower edge.

Stuff the paws but not the arms with wool. Sew together both red tongue pieces, leaving the straight edge open. Trim the seam allowance and turn the tongue right side out. Insert the tongue between the base of the two mouth pieces and sew right across (Figure 3).

Lay the face and back of head pieces together, right sides facing, and sew the cheeks and ears together, from C to D (Figure 4). Place the face against the throat, right sides facing, and sew, from C to E and from D to F (Figure 5).

Open the grey mouth and insert the red tongue, right sides facing (the tongue will point inwards into the head). Sew all around the mouth, upper and lower jaws, from C to D (Figure 6).

Turn the head right side out. Sew a couple of stitches across the base of each ear so that they are not filled with wool. Stuff the head but leave room inside the mouth for your fingers.

Using two pieces of yellow felt, sew on slanted eyes with black pupils, or embroider the eyes. Embroider a black nose. Sew the head to the body with strong thread. Sew claws in the form of large eyelets on the paws (Figure 7).

Head pieces in grey

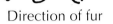

Direction of fur

Mouth and tongue in red

1

Leave
open

A   A

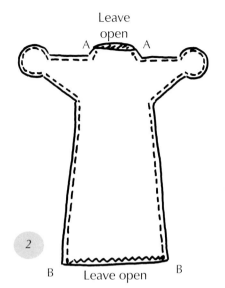

B   B
Leave open

2

3

C   D

4

C   D

E   F

5

C   D

6

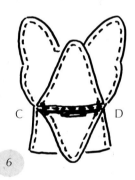

7

107

WOLF

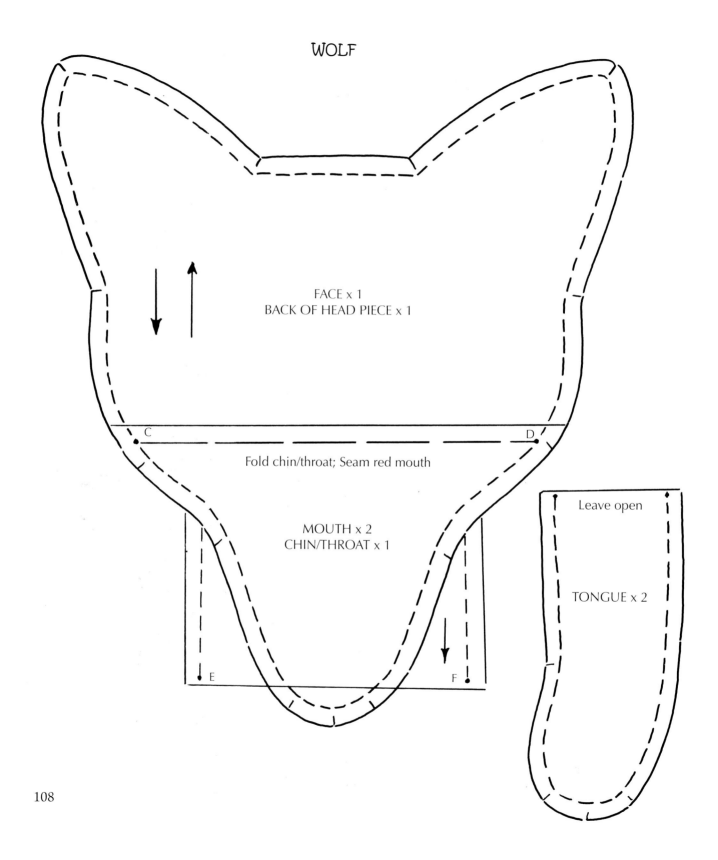

FACE x 1
BACK OF HEAD PIECE x 1

C   D

Fold chin/throat; Seam red mouth

MOUTH x 2
CHIN/THROAT x 1

E   F

Leave open

TONGUE x 2

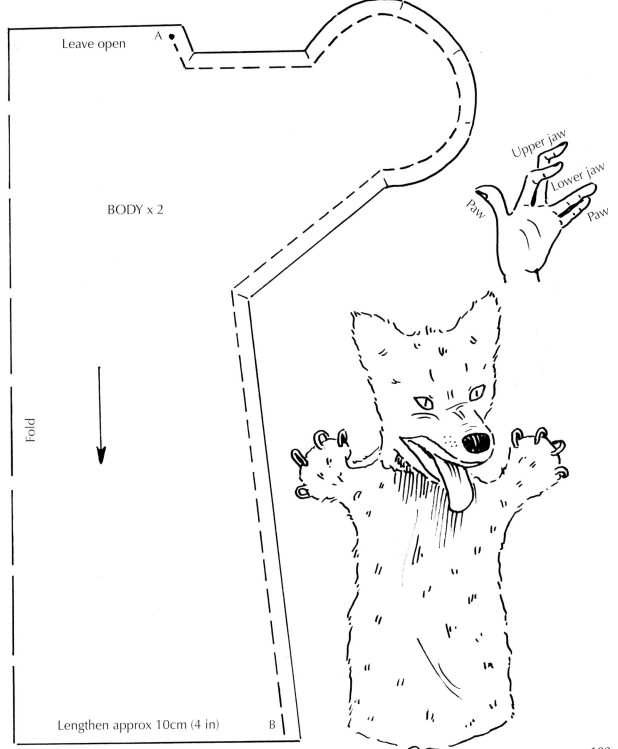

Leave open

A

BODY x 2

Fold

Lengthen approx 10cm (4 in)

B

Upper jaw

Lower jaw

Paw

Paw

Further reading

Adolphi, Sybille, *Making Fairy Tale Scenes,*
  Floris Books, Edinburgh.
—, *Making Flower Children,* Floris Books, Edinburgh.
—, *Making More Flower Children,* Floris Books,
  Edinburgh.
Anschütz, Marieke, *Children and their Temperaments,*
  Floris Books, Edinburgh.
Berger, Petra, *Feltcraft,* Floris Books, Edinburgh.
Berger, Thomas, *The Christmas Craft Book,*
  Floris Books, Edinburgh.
Berger, Thomas & Petra, *Crafts through the Year,*
  Floris Books, Edinburgh.
—, *The Gnome Craft Book,* Floris Books, Edinburgh.
Clouder, Chris & Martyn Rawson, *Waldorf Education,*
  Floris Books, Edinburgh.
Crossley, Diana, *Muddles, Puddles and Sunshine,*
  Hawthorn Press, Stroud.
Dancy, Rahima Baldwin, *You are your Child's First
  Teacher,* Celestial Arts.
Dhom, Christel, *The Advent Craft and Activity Book,*
  Floris Books, Edinburgh.
Evans, Russell, *Helping Children to Overcome Fear,*
  Hawthorn Press, Stroud.
Frommherz, Andrea & Edith Biedermann, *The
  Wonder of Trees,* Floris Books, Edinburgh.
Grunelius, Elisabeth, *Early Childhood Education and
  the Waldorf School Plan,* Waldorf Monographs,
  New York.
Guéret, Frédérique, *Magical Window Stars,*
  Floris Books, Edinburgh.

Harwood, A.C. *The Way of a Child,* Steiner Press,
  London.
Jaffke, Freya, *Celebrating Festivals with Children,* Floris
  Books, Edinburgh.
—, *Toymaking with Children,* Floris Books,
Edinburgh.
—, *Work and Play in Early Childhood,* Floris Books,
  Edinburgh.
Jaffke, Freya & Dagmar Schmidt, *Magic Wool,* Floris
  Books, Edinburgh.
Jenkinson, Sally, *The Genius of Play,* Hawthorn Press,
  Stroud.
König, Karl, *The First Three Years of the Child,*
  Floris Books, Edinburgh.
Kornberger, Horst, *The Power of Stories,* Floris Books,
  Edinburgh.
Kutsch, Irmgard & Brigitte Walden, *Autumn Nature
  Activities for Children,* Floris Books, Edinburgh.
—, *Spring Nature Activities for Children,* Floris Books,
  Edinburgh.
—, *Summer Nature Activities for Children,*
  Floris Books, Edinburgh.
—, *Winter Nature Activities for Chidren,*
  Floris Books, Edinburgh.
Kraul, Walter, *Earth, Water, Fire and Air,* Floris Books,
  Edinburgh.
Leeuwen, M van & J Moeskops, *The Nature Corner,*
  Floris Books, Edinburgh.
Lochie, Beatrys, *Bedtime Storytelling,* Floris Books,
  Edinburgh

Mellon, Nancy, *Storytelling with Children,* Hawthorn Press, Stroud.

Meyer, Rudolf, *The Wisdom of Fairy Tales,* Floris Books, Edinburgh.

Müller, Brunhild, *Painting with Children,* Floris Books, Edinburgh.

Neuschütz, Karin, *Creative Wool,* Floris Books, Edinburgh.

—, *Sewing Dolls,* Floris Books, Edinburgh.

Oldfield, Lynne, *Free to Learn,* Hawthorn Press, Stroud.

Petrash, Carol, *Earthwise: Environmental Crafts and Activities with Young Children,* Floris Books, Edinburgh & Gryphon House, Maryland.

Rawson, Martyn & Michael Rose, *Ready to Learn,* Hawthorn Press, Stroud.

Reinckens, Sunnhild, *Making Dolls,* Floris Books, Edinburgh.

Reinhard, Rotraud, *A Felt Farm,* Floris Books, Edinburgh.

Santer, Ivor, *Green Fingers and Muddy Boots,* Floris Books, Edinburgh.

Schäfer, Christine, *Magic Wool Fairies*, Floris Books, Edinburgh.

Schmidt, Dagmar & Freya Jaffke, *Magic Wool,* Floris Books, Edinburgh.

Sealey, Maricristin, *Kinder Dolls,* Hawthorn Press, Stroud.

Steiner, Rudolf, *The Education of the Child in the Light of Anthroposophy,* Steiner Press, London, & Anthroposophic Press, New York.

Taylor, Michael, *Finger Strings,* Floris Books, Edinburgh.

Thomas, Anne & Peter, *The Children's Party Book,* Floris Books, Edinburgh.

Wolck-Gerche, Angelika, *Creative Felt,* Floris Books, Edinburgh.

—, *More Magic Wool,* Floris Books, Edinburgh.

—, *Papercraft,* Floris Books, Edinburgh.

Resources

SOURCES FOR MAGIC WOOL AND NATURAL
MATERIALS

AUSTRALIA
Morning Star
www.morningstarcrafts.com.au

Winterwood Toys
www.winterwoodtoys.com.au

NORTH AMERICA
The Waldorf Early Childhood Association of North
America maintains an online list of suppliers at:
www.waldorfearlychildhood.org/sources.asp

UK
Myriad Natural Toys
www.myriadonline.co.uk

STEINER-WALDORF SCHOOLS

In 2012 there are over 1000 Waldorf schools and
1,500 kindergartens in over 60 countries around the
world. Up-to-date information can be found on any of
the websites below.

AUSTRALIA
Steiner Education Australia, 6/73 Albert Avenue,
Chatswood, NSW 2067
sea@steineroz.com
www.steinereducation.edu.au

NEW ZEALAND
Federation of Rudolf Steiner Schools, PO Box 888,
Hastings, Hawkes Bay
steiner.federation@gmail.com
www.rudolfsteinerfederation.org.nz

NORTH AMERICA
Association of Waldorf Schools of North America,
3911 Bannister Road, Fair Oaks, CA 95628
awsna@awsna.org
www.whywaldorfworks.org

SOUTH AFRICA
Southern African Federation of Waldorf Schools,
McGregor House, 4 Victoria Road, Plumstead 7800,
Cape Town
info@waldorf.org.za
www.waldorf.org.za

UK
Steiner Waldorf Schools Fellowship, 10 Church Street,
Stourbridge DY8 1LT
admin@swsf.org.uk
www.steinerwaldorf.org.uk

KARIN NEUSCHUTZ

www.karinneuschtz.se